About th

Solara An-Ra is a global leader in the transformation of our civilisation and planet. Over-lighted by advanced star beings in her early youth, her life has been a guided, dedicated, gift to us all. Through her offerings as a direct-voice channel, seekers across the planet have come to know and love members of the Councils of Light, who come from higher dimensional star systems, including the Pleiades, Sirius, Arcturus and Andromeda.

Solara shares channelled messages and meditations from the Star Councils with over 33,000 subscribers on her YouTube channel and website, providing guidance, tools and community to a world searching for meaning. She has a combined download/view count of over 6 million for the guided meditations that she provides freely, teaching vital skills towards manifesting an empowered, fulfilling and heart-centred life. Her website acts as a portal, proffering the wisdom that she has accessed on her path of service to the people of Earth; the *Light Tribe of Gaia.*

For many years Solara travelled the globe, alone and with groups, opening portals and reactivating sacred sites in order to reinstate a long-awaited "Golden Age" on our planet. Now in the quieter *Magic Weaver* phase of her life, she serves from the Centre of Light she has created on the island of Ibiza, teaching and hosting spiritual groups from her new home. The story she shares here, with her characteristic sense of humour and honesty, is yet another gift to the tribe. It is a reminder to all of us that the universe has a few tricks up its sleeve when it comes to waking us up. It will invariably shake us out of our complacency by landing us in the eye of the hurricane – and just when we think all is lost, we find a way into the peace and power which is our birth-right.

One-Heart is a publishing company designed to bring
5th dimensional consciousness to Earth.

People may quote from this book with pleasure as long as reference is made
to Solara An-Ra's work & website. To receive news of further books, plus new
channelled messages and meditations, please subscribe to Solara's newsletter on:

www.solara.org.uk

For teaching videos, guided meditations and channelled messages, subscribe to
Solara An-Ra's YouTube Channel:

www.youtube.com/user/SolaraAnRa

ISBN 978-0-9956688-0-5

Editorial assistance: Gabby Zahara & Sadhya Moss
Cover & layout design by candydesign.studio

PLEIADIAN EMISSARY TO GAIA

A Journey Between Worlds

SOLARA AN-RA

Contents

PART 5 ~ WARRIOR OF THE LIGHT

PART 6 ~ RECONNECTING THE CODES

PART 7 ~ MAGIC WEAVER

Introduction
by Solara An-Ra

I was never into UFO's or extraterrestrials. The simple fact is that when I became aware of the crucial transformation through which Earth was going – and committed to being of service – the star people heard my call. Unbeknownst to me, I had made an agreement with the P's at the tender age of four to be a *Pleiadian Emissary to Gaia,* and they held me to it.

My commitment to assisting with the evolution of our planet was not entirely altruistic, for I had a lot to gain from a new and improved experience of life on Earth. As a child and young adult, I was deeply unhappy; I felt isolated, and above all else, I was excruciatingly *bored!* My connection with the star beings was – and continues to be – the most exciting and joyful influence in my life. The fact that I became a leader and teacher for so many is down to the unfailing guidance and assistance that I received from them.

I dedicate this book to the Star Councils of Light – my dear Pleiadian, Andromedan, Sirian and Arcturian friends. Their patience for our process is infinite; their kindness and compassion, deeply touching. Without these wonderful teachers and allies, I would still be stuck in the avoidance and powerlessness of my early years.

Our DNA is seeded by star beings – all indigenous cultures on our planet knew this, and acknowledged their star-seed ancestry in their most ancient myths and artwork. As a race, we are now in the process of remembering our connection with the stars. The quantum leap that we are making in this time window is like stepping off the edge of the world. Just as Galileo struggled to persuade the people of his time that there *was* no edge, so must we collectively let go of our fears about our uncertain future, and believe that our continued existence beyond the third- dimensional world is our highest and most joy-ful destination.

The Star Councils assure us that, as difficult as we might sometimes find our Earth journey, our evolution is in progress, along with that of all other life forms on our beautiful planet. The trick is to *trust that this is so,* and then to enjoy the ride.

There is a reason that you are reading these words. You have chosen to be right here, right now, to assist your human tribe and planet through the transition, and you have called on a soul level for a reminder of this purpose. Say out loud:

I let go of all resistance to change.

I am a co-creator in the Divine Plan for Ascension of Gaia.

I step fearlessly into the new Age of Light!

Your process has begun.

PART 1

The Beginning

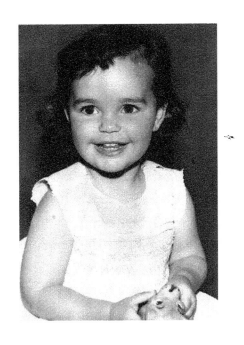

CHAPTER 1
The Meaning of Life

Many years ago, my friends and family encouraged me to write a book about my travels – a period of my life, fresh out of university, when I back-packed more or less penniless through a random set of countries around the globe. When I left South Africa for Israel at the age of nineteen I had planned to be away for three months over the summer break. Three months grew into three long years as I drifted from one country to the next, always in the hope that just around the corner I might find the meaning of life, the universe and everything.

It did appeal to me to write a book, but what stopped me was the fear that the adventures I'd had weren't actually that interesting – certainly not as fascinating as I'd made out at the time! Sure, I could write an amusing yarn, but what would be the point? I'd be repeating the exaggerations and half-lies that had filled the postcards I'd sent home. My postcards had spoken of the excitement of exotic places and were full of Bill Bryson-style anecdotes about my weird and wacky overseas escapades. I had developed a pattern of needing to be entertaining, so it never occurred to me to be honest about the times that were depressing, frightening, or just downright boring. After all, I had an obligation to be enjoying myself, if for no other reason than – I was travelling the world!

There were long periods where an honest account might have read: "Dear Mom and Dad, I'm back in the States again, bored out of my mind. My boyfriend sucks, but I'm still clinging onto him in case there's no one better around the corner. Earning minimum wage cleaning motel toilets by day and serving fast food by night is unutterably depressing. I just can't face the prospect of coming home and having to decide on a real career that will live up to your expectations of me!"

You get the picture.

As I've awakened, I've realised that my greatest adventures haven't necessarily involved travelling. Every single situation I've attracted to myself, every person I've encountered along the way, has been pivotal in the grand ongoing quest which is my life. I now understand the universal laws of creation – an understanding that assists me in realigning when my life is out of synch. My deepest wish, dear reader, is that my story will allow you to take a short-cut to understanding the meaning of life.

When the time was right, the decision to write or not write this book was taken out of my hands. My guides were so adamant that my tale be documented, I had no option but to comply. They explained:

> In the telling of your story you come to completion, dear one. You birth a new chapter – a well-deserved immersion into peace and integration. And in the reading of your journey of awakening there is of course purpose for your audience also. Many will resonate with your journey; your words will echo their feelings and their experiences, as they travel the road of Earth life alongside you. Your lessons are their lessons also; your completions will assist in their completions; your realisations will assist in their awakening process.

In other words, I was told that the completion and publication of this book was essential for my own healing. Without this, I would not be able to enter into the long-awaited phase of my life in which I was to be rewarded with total peace and relaxation. Any benefits that you receive from reading my chronicle are, apparently, an added bonus.

But let's start at the very beginning – a very good place to start, according to the singing nun in *The Sound of Music*.

CHAPTER 2
Pleiadian Playdate

I was born on the 24th of July 1958 in Cape Town, South Africa; the third girl to see the light of day from my mother's traumatised womb. She had been warned by her doctor after the difficult birth of her second daughter that having another child would constitute a risk to her life. But when she fell pregnant again, by "mistake," she decided to take that risk. My poor mother had suffered the stillbirth of twin boys during her very first pregnancy, and had always longed for a son. I guess she hoped that her boy might finally arrive. Not only was I to disappoint her on that front, my birth *did* very nearly kill her, as predicted.

My mum was so ill after my birth that she needed full time care for several months. Rather than have her stay in hospital, my dad drove the whole family to East London, up the coast from Cape Town, to stay at her parents' home. Christened "Gillian Eva Sheer," my middle name came from this grandmother, with whom I was to spend the first days of my life. Eva was a tough Aussie bird, mother of ten children, and a firm advocate of the principle that children should be seen and not heard. I can only imagine the military-style organisation necessary to accommodate her critically ill daughter, my two toddler sisters and the new-born baby – me!

My grandfather, Hendrik, was put in charge of me. I have no memories of him because he died when I was young, but I am told that he was a gentle and sweet Afrikaner-born man who worked on the railway. My mother never volunteered much information about our births or childhoods, and I only discovered Hendrik's role in my life when I had a reading from a "medium" at the London College of Psychic Studies in the late eighties.* During the reading I received a message from a relative whose name wasn't quite clear – the closest

---

* A medium is a person who is able to make contact with "the other side," transmitting messages from those who have passed over.

approximation the medium could make was "Henry." The message was that he had felt like a real father to me, and that he was very proud of my progress. He added that I would reach an understanding of life far deeper than he had ever achieved in his lifetime.

Puzzled, I phoned my mom after the reading to ask if there could be a relative called Henry who might think of me as his own child. "Oh yes," she said casually, "Henry is the English version of Hendrik. My father Hendrik looked after you for the first few months of your life while I was ill."

I was incredulous that I had never been told about my grandfather's role in my infant months! My shock was tempered by my excitement at the validation of the message from the spirit worlds via Hendrik. This was before my connection with my own guides – a period in the eighties when I visited psychics and mediums regularly and was increasingly fascinated by the process of channelling.

My parents moved from Cape Town to Johannesburg soon after my mother regained her strength. They bought a half-acre plot of land in a respectable suburb and set about building their dream house. Both my mother and father had worked tirelessly to rise above their poverty-stricken backgrounds. Manifesting a four-bedroom house with a swimming pool and spacious garden was a massive achievement for them.

My father was a man of remarkable determination. He started life at an extreme disadvantage, losing his mother at a young age and subsequently being separated from his alcoholic father after he re-married. Relocated to his aunt's over-crowded home in Johannesburg, my father was squashed into a room with several cousins. A clever boy, he skipped two grades at school, graduating at the tender age of sixteen. For the following three years he attended the University of Witwatersrand, funding his accounting degree by working part-time. As there was no space or quiet to study at home, he adopted the habit of doing his coursework at night on a park bench by the light of a street lamp. By nineteen he was a qualified chartered accountant, and by the time I came into the world he had made himself into a successful businessman.

My mother was happiest in the intervals in which she worked as a nursing sister, a vocation in which she found purpose and strength. When she quit her job in order to be a full-time mum, she lapsed into the depression which haunted her through most of her adult life. She devoted herself to creating a beautiful garden and to putting on a show in which she starred as a good mother and wife. But the truth of the matter was that my parents were often in conflict – usually about how much money my mother was spending or how much alcohol my father was drinking.

We three sisters, self-centred in the way that children often are, dismissed their concerns and focussed on our own interests. We took our privileged life for granted – we knew nothing else. Growing up in the heyday of Apartheid, we lived a typical South African middle class existence, with a live-in maid and twice-a-week gardener. We played in our swimming pool with the neighbourhood kids after school; took tennis and drama lessons; and obsessed about boys, fashion and parties.

My strongest memories of my oldest sister Gail are like a Mary Quant ad from the late sixties: miniskirts, glamorous false eyelashes and pale pink lipstick. My dad would fake a heart attack every time she appeared in a new miniskirt, threatening to lock her up so she couldn't leave the house indecently dressed. Hair straighteners hadn't been invented back then, so she would employ me to iron her hair under a tea towel on the ironing board. As soon as she passed her secretarial diploma, Gail left the house – off to her first apartment in Hillbrow and the working girl's world.

My middle sister Darrell and I were often at odds with each other, if not actually fighting like wild cats. This was fuelled by my mother constantly praising me and comparing the two of us – not an approach likely to build confidence in a middle child. Darrell became the rebel of the family, insisting on going to boarding school out in the sticks to escape home. She cut off her long blonde locks, started smoking grass, and would sometimes steal my mother's car to go joyriding – a sin almost punishable by death, with a father as strict as ours.

I was living two separate lives. On the outside, I looked like a cheerful little girl, enduring the routines of family and social life without complaint. I was healthy, confident, did well at school and sports, and had lots of friends. On the inside, however, I was deeply unhappy. I wasn't *connected* to anyone or anything. I felt like I was an actor in a drama, in which if I smiled, made the right moves and spoke the appropriate words, no one would notice I didn't belong. I had no idea if anyone else felt the same way and I didn't dare ask, lest I was found out to be an imposter.

Even in the most extreme circumstances, such as when my parents proposed to divorce or when my mother attempted suicide, I felt emotionally detached. I was in a TV drama, performing the role that was expected of me. The strangest thing was that no one seemed to be aware that I didn't fit in – that I was an alien.

The time of day I treasured most was the early dawn before the house was awake, when I would jump out of my bedroom window onto the lawn and slide into the cool blue water of our swimming pool. My favourite thing to do was to dive down in the deep end, hold my breath and watch as the rising sun created geometric patterns on the water surface. I was in another world – a world of sparkling, shifting, blue and white light which I somehow remembered from another existence.

I also found solace escaping into the room of our Zulu maid, in our back garden – a place where neither my sisters nor parents ever ventured. The cruel Apartheid laws stipulated that servants' quarters had to be a restricted size, with small windows, and that maids must live alone whether married or not. Katy's room was a box of unpainted concrete blocks and was imbued with a strange but not unpleasant smell – a mixture of sour-milk *mieliepap*, candlewax and the starched linen of her Zion church robes.

Katy liked me visiting her, and would lift me onto her bed which was raised up high on piles of bricks so that the *tokoloshe* couldn't get her in her sleep. These mythical child-sized gremlins, said to be created by shamans from dead bodies, were very real to the Zulu and Xhosa tribes. When I asked her to tell me about the tokoloshe, her eyes would widen in fear at the very thought of the creatures. I loved the mystery of her beliefs and culture, so very different from white South Africans, and the element of magic in her stories. Katy's life felt *real* to me – her struggles and joys meaningful.

You will learn as my story unfolds how I came to be a "channel" for the Pleiadians – able to bring through information from these higher dimensional star beings. It was through this means that I finally received an explanation as to why I had felt so strangely disconnected in my childhood. I was told by my Pleiadian guides that, at the age of four, I had been taken from the garden of my childhood home onto a spaceship. Something happened on that ship which disconnected me from my family. Akin to a "walk-in" experience, I found myself after the incident living in a reality to which I couldn't relate; learning from scratch how to fit in and survive.*

The transmissions from these Pleiadian guides came initially in the form of child-like poems, which I sang rather than spoke. As I channelled the first message into my recorder, I was transfixed by the singing and by the fact that the lines of the message rhymed. My attention was distracted away from the actual information I was being given, which stopped me from going into protest. Fearful of the abduction implications, I was certainly not ready to hear about my spaceship experience – it brought up too many disturbing questions.

Had the incident been removed from my memory bank with a *Men-in-Black* type device? Or had I forgotten about it because there was no way of integrating it into my life? And why was I only being told about it at this juncture? My guides were infinitely patient with me, and the pieces of the puzzle slowly slotted into place over the following year, culminating in a vivid flashback memory of the event during a rebirthing session. The memory was so astonishingly

---

* A walk-in experience involves one soul moving into the body of another soul who has chosen to leave the planet. It is a mutual agreement between the two, but it can be very disorientating for the new soul to adapt to life in a body without having actually gone through the process of being born and growing up.

real that it dissolved my doubts and also my fears. If you have ever experienced a spontaneous flashback, you will understand that it's not like a dream – it is a movement backwards in time where you are reliving the actual incident as it takes place.

In the flashback I was a small child in a white dress with long dark hair down my back, standing on the big lawn in front of our house. I was looking up at a spaceship from which a beam of light emanated, hearing a telepathic message inviting me up to play. I glanced around at my mother gardening and my father on the verandah, realising that no one else could see the ship, and it made me giggle. With no hesitation I answered "Yes!" And in an instant I had entered the beam of light, and then the ship itself.

I smiled in wonder at these new friends, marvelling that we could speak to each other without words. Everything glowed: the fabric of the ship, the panels of technical equipment set into the walls and the light people themselves – I could see the energy in everything. We were seated in a large round space on semi-circular benches and I answered many questions, allowing them access to my mind. I was made to understand that this meeting was important and that an agreement was being made between us. The next minute I was back on the lawn, disorientated and tearful at being wrenched away from my new friends. As the flashback faded away, I felt myself in my adult body and in the rebirthing room once again.

After the session, I was told by my guides that when the timing was right I would understand why my Pleiadian playdate had resulted in my disconnection from the 3-D (third-dimensional) world. For the moment, they explained, it was enough for me to know that my extrication from the emotional fabric of my family had served an important purpose. It had made it easier for me to focus on my spiritual path and to connect with the higher dimensional worlds. Ultimately it proved to be the very gift which allowed me to assume the role my guides gave me: *Pleiadian Emissary to Gaia*.

But I am getting ahead of myself again. Let us return to my early years on this planet; and the chronicle of my journey between worlds will unfold in its own time.

My grandparents, Hendrik & Eva

Mom & Dad on honeymoon

The three Sheer girls

The only photo I have of Katy

Aged 4 with Darrell

School photo: aged 6

Gail's wedding - Darrell & I as bridesmaids

CHAPTER 3

Boyfriend Pick-and-Mix

My history with the opposite sex began at the tender age of eleven, and the whole phenomenon of boy-meets-girl grabbed my attention one hundred percent. This was outside of family life and rules – a realm of chance, danger and passion. Love relationships presented me with an opportunity to experiment with real emotional connection, and I dedicated myself to the mating game with a genuine fervour.

My junior school had a built-in dating system with a strict set of rules. From a girl's perspective these were: (1) You must be in grade four (aged eleven) in order to begin dating. (2) The boy always makes the first move, the most common move being to buy the chosen girl an ice cream at break-time. (3) If this gesture is accepted, the boy makes the second move by buying you a ticket for Friday movies in the school hall, known in South Africa as the "Friday night flick." (4) You hold hands during the movie and finish the evening with a quick kiss – made more exciting by the presence of a teacher who continually prowls the aisles with a torch to inhibit illegal necking.

Hanging out with your boyfriend outside of movie nights was not particularly rewarding in grade four – it seemed as though there was no structure in place for how to relate, when boys and girls played different games and liked different things. But in grade five, aged twelve, a thrilling new phase was initiated when we started to have "mixed birthday parties." These ushered in a whole new dimension of boy-girl interaction in the form of slow dancing, and kissing games.

Slow dancing involved clinging awkwardly onto your boyfriend, while shuffling around the cement floor of someone's garage to the strains of *My Belle Amie*. Nevertheless, in the presence of rising hormones on both sides it was our introduction to being intimate with the opposite sex; a whole new adventure. Equally exciting was the game *Spin the Bottle,* in which you could kiss any of several boys, according to where the bottle landed! The sexist system that was set up at our school meant that girls only had the choice of the boys who approached them, and by twelve I was already busting to break the rules. I was waking up to the fact that some boys were much more attractive to me than others, and I was determined to make my own choices from then on.

By the age of thirteen I was unusually mature on a physical and emotional level and was mixing with older guys. I met my first serious boyfriend, Steve, and fell in love for the first time. I can't imagine why my parents let me go out with Steve – he was nearly four years older than me, with long hair, a motorbike and a naughty grin. In his favour, he was an extremely charming chap, and very respectful to my mom and dad. He scored points by mowing the lawn, and by calling my dad "Mr. Sheer" in the old fashioned South African way – respect for elders and all that.

The amount of freedom I was given at that young age was probably due to my being the third child. My parents were exhausted after seeing my two older sisters through puberty and trying to keep them out of trouble. Even at thirteen I managed to give the impression that I was independent and responsible; that I could look after myself. Relieved and preoccupied, my parents bought into that notion, leaving me to my own devices.

As I was not allowed on Steve's bike, he would borrow his mate's car, pick me up, and then drive a few blocks away to where his friend was waiting with his bike. We'd swap over and zoom off on the bike, often returning to the house in the wee hours of the morning, when I would sneak into the house through my bedroom window. I had finally entered a world that was real to me; a world of love, caring, spontaneity and fun. I set up a pattern that was to dictate my life for decades to come, in which my romantic partnership always came first. I believed that this was the only avenue through which true love and connection was accessible to me.

A year into our relationship Steve was drafted into the army, and for a few months I used all my pocket money to send care parcels to his base camp. But a fifteen-year-old girl can only maintain a long-distance liaison for so long when other boys are knocking at the door, and I soon had another love in my life. Boyfriends were my emotional succour and my escape ticket from domesticity and suburbia.

At seventeen I attained my freedom for real when I left Johannesburg to do an Arts Degree at Cape Town University. I had insisted that if I was to study further it must be in Cape Town, as far away from Jo'burg as I could get. The city, I had heard, was flanked by beaches, mountains and forests on all sides.

I fell in love with Cape Town instantly. I was also in love with a new man; one who felt like a soulmate. Mark and I were inseparable in our first six months of university. We met in the cafeteria between lectures, spent whole days on the beach, shared pizza in our favourite hangout, and were locked in each other's arms in every possible waking moment.

I had made a deal with my parents to stay in an all-girls student residence, but sharing a room with a very prim and proper girl and having a no-boys-in-rooms policy felt like incarceration. A few months into the year I conspired to get kicked out of halls by having Mark climb up the outside of the building into my room. My parents shrugged their shoulders and let me do what I'd wanted to all along, which was to move into a shared house. I was totally independent at last! I was also about to experience my first heartbreak.

There were no warning signs leading to Mark's break-up speech. Trusting his dedication to me implicitly, I was oblivious to his wandering eyes and waning attention. When he told me he wanted out, I was devastated. I literally cried for months. To be truly broken-hearted is not only an emotional experience – I felt as though my physical heart was ripped open and bleeding. I had broken a few hearts along the way, but it was the first time it had happened to me.

When I ventured out into the land of the living again, I needed a radical change to reignite my enthusiasm for life. It was the late seventies – high time to get into the hippy thing and break away from the middle class crew with whom I'd been hanging out, Mark included. Over the summer break, after telling my family I was staying in Cape Town to do a project, I secretly hitchhiked with my university friend Lindsey all the way up the West African coast to Swakopmund in Namibia. It was a dangerous journey for two young girls, a hairy 1,300 kilometre trek through isolated territory. Our experience was frightening in parts, but the exhilaration of being out on the open road left us determined to explore more of the world when the opportunity presented itself.

On our return to Cape Town I moved into a ramshackle house on the wrong side of the tracks with some grass-smoking surfer-dudes. I had decided that surfers were *it*. I turned vegetarian, listened to Pink Floyd, Joni Mitchell and Bob Dylan, and went hang gliding or surfing with the crew every weekend. I fulfilled the role of every good surfer-groupie chick – taking photos of the guys, hanging out looking sexy on the beach, and making tea and toast in the obligatory campervan. I joined in when the crew went skateboarding, the alternative surfer-cool activity when the winds were blowing the wrong way.

I will tell one more boyfriend story here, because of the potent lesson it taught me. The man in question was one of my housemates, a rather miniature but cute flute-playing surfer with long blonde hair, nicknamed "Midge." He was a real eccentric, which was massively attractive to me, but was also rather shy. After flirting with him for weeks with no tangible results, I went for the direct approach and inserted myself into his bed one night. The rest was history.

The weird part was that we were never openly an item, even though most of our friends knew we were seeing each other. We never held hands or were physical outside of the bedroom, and I assumed he didn't think it was cool to be affectionate in public. I played along with this game, although the whole situation was torture for me – I was longing for the kind of open, loving partnership I'd had previously. Our liaison came to a painful and inconclusive end when I left Cape Town and started my travels abroad. Here comes the interesting bit.

Thirteen years later when I was married, pregnant, and living in London, I came across Midge, by some bizarre twist of fate, jogging down the road I lived on! He was in London to attend an ecological conference, and we ended up having tea and chatting for hours. This first real, honest conversation that had ever passed between us blew my mind.

Midge thanked me for helping him overcome his shyness with women, confirming my suspicion that I had been his first sexual partner. He added that he would never have been able to approach the girl who'd since become his wife had I not been so kind in teaching him the ways of love. I discovered, to my absolute astonishment, that he'd assumed that *I* was the one who wanted to keep our relationship private, because *I* was so cool.

We had suffered all that pain and awkwardness for a year and a half, both of us completely misreading each other's feelings, when just one honest conversation would have sorted it out! This is a perfect example of one of the powerful Toltec teachings from Don Miguel Ruiz's book *The Four Agreements*. The lesson I learned in this encounter with an old flame was one of the four agreements Toltec warriors agree to live by: *Never make assumptions.*

Never assume you know what someone is thinking or feeling, dear reader, even your best friend or long-term lover. Just open your heart, allow yourself to be vulnerable, and talk about it. It will revolutionise your relationships.

Skateboarding tomboy

With the animals in the garden

On Llundudno beach

In Rondebosch forest, Cape Town

Hiking to Namibia with Lindsey

Pochontas playing the flute

CHAPTER 4
Globe Trotting

D ecember 1978 found me at the end of my B.A. degree, extremely worried about whether I'd passed the final exams after spending most of the year on the beach, rather than in lectures. Perpetually broke in classic student style, Lindsey and I were looking for the cheapest escape route from South Africa for the summer holidays. My tentative plan, in the event that I *had* passed my exams, was to return to university after the three-month break to do an add-on teaching diploma.

Staying on a kibbutz seemed like the perfect solution; the flights to Israel were the cheapest we could find to an overseas destination, and kibbutz life apparently involved no responsibilities beyond four hours of farm labour per day. Everything was provided: accommodation, food, clothes, cigarettes, tampons, and a bit of pocket money to squander as you chose. It sounded ideal – an undertaking which was worlds away from South Africa, studying and parents. It also promised a potential bonus in the form of exciting foreign boyfriends.

Having arrived in Tel Aviv, it never occurred to Lindsey and I to do anything other than hitchhike to our chosen kibbutz. We had hiked our way around Cape Town for years – to the beach, to friends' houses, to university; not to mention our infamous hike to Swakopmund. Our adventure in Israel thus began in an army truck, bumping along dusty roads towards Kibbutz Nir David, a ride which had us surrounded by curious, gun-wielding young soldiers.

On the kibbutz we were grouped together with about twenty other foreigners under the category of "volunteers" who were needed for physical labour because of the migration of young kibbutzniks to the towns. There was a second group of temporary residents called the "Ulpan," made up primarily of young Jewish Americans learning Hebrew in their college break. Together we made an interesting, eclectic bunch – an eighteen-to-thirties crew of different nationalities, thrown together by our mutual non-belonging.

There was a Vietnam veteran by the name of Terry who was the mafia element of the volunteers – trading favours and luxuries that weren't provided, such as wine and chocolate, for participation in his hash parties. I was fascinated at first by the decadent illicit evenings in Terry's room. We would light a block of hash on a pin pushed through a matchbox, which in turn was placed inside an inverted glass teacup on a saucer. Each one in the circle would wait for the cup to fill with smoke, inhale the smoke from under the edge, and pass it on to the next person.

The reality of the parties, however, wasn't as glamorous as the idea. I would find myself in a roomful of monged-out foreigners, too paranoid to speak. The munchies that inevitably ensued would lead to our climbing over the locked gate into the kitchen area in search of creamy yoghurts, matzos and honey. The end result – putting on several extra kilos and enduring horrible day-after headaches – was not so attractive.

I was intrigued by a group of seemingly introverted Scandinavian girls amongst the volunteer group who showed a totally different side to their personalities when drunk. Friday night marked the official beginning of the weekend, and was therefore "party night" on the kibbutz. The young Danish and Norwegian girls would get wildly drunk and then pick a willing guy to take to bed, apparently at random. I was amazed by their promiscuity and by the lack of guilt or obligation that accompanied it. They weren't after boyfriends – they were just having fun! My pattern with the opposite sex was very different. For me, sex was part of the ritual of acquiring a *real* boyfriend.

It didn't take long for me to hook up with a mellow West Coast Yankee with long golden-red hair – men with long hair being a weakness of mine. Gary was sweet-natured and kind, and he helped heal the pain of my separation from Midge. I needed to be wanted, and he wanted me.

Lindsey left the kibbutz after three months, returning to university as planned. To my surprise I had passed my final year, but I couldn't face going home and having to decide on a career. Of the three children in my family I was the only one my parents had put through uni, which meant that I was expected to do something worthwhile – and I had no idea what that might be. I opted in the meantime for the easy life of the kibbutz; enjoying the physical work in the grapefruit, olive or avocado fields; and the lazy days with no agenda. There was some leeway with our working hours, and our gang selected the early shift, from 4 till 8 a.m. That way we had the rest of the day free to hang out by the river and go walking in the hills.

After six months, however, when Gary and I were given the option to officially join the commune, I questioned if I belonged there. The original founders of the kibbutz were members of a political youth movement formed in the aftermath of the Second World War. The organisation had accepted over a hundred Holocaust survivors and had been founded on socialist principles. Both the older and younger members held fast to their political stance – everything shared, everything equal. Where was there room for me to grow there, rather than just survive?

I am not a political animal – never have been, never will be. I burnt a piece of hair once in a demonstration at uni, but I don't think that counts, as I can't even remember the point of the protest. I certainly wasn't a socialist. More significantly, I realised that escaping to a no-effort zone wasn't enough for me. Maybe I didn't want my family's expectations hanging over me, but I did want to do *something* with my life. It was time to move on.

The cheapest way to move west from Israel at that time was to sleep under the stars on the deck of a Greece-bound ferry. Does that sound romantic? Suffice it to say that anyone who has a problem with festival toilets would have had to consider jumping overboard on that journey. Being crammed into a restricted area with no escape but the Atlantic

Sleeping deck-class on the ferry to Greece

Ocean, with dozens of sea-sick passengers and very few toilets, is as unromantic an experience as you're ever likely to have. The toilets were dysfunctional within hours of our departure and stayed that way for the remaining twelve hours. Little did I suspect that I was about to enter a period of my travels where toilets would feature quite significantly.

I had saved enough of my pocket money in Israel to be a tourist for a while, and my university friend Rosy joined me in Greece for a month of island-hopping. We sailed between islands, lay in the sun, swam in the wonderful Mediterranean Sea, and ate an obscene amount of baklava – the sticky honey-drenched pastry traditionally served with Greek coffee. When my funds ran out I worked in a youth hostel in Athens for a while, but the noise and chaos of the city proved too much for me after the rural life of the kibbutz.

As an unskilled foreigner, employment options in most of the countries I visited were restricted to farm labour, waitressing, cleaning (in various degrees of unpleasantness) or kitchen work. On the kibbutz I'd enjoyed the hardy outdoor work, but that option wasn't always available in other destinations.

In Greece I finally found a job working as a maid in a tourist hotel on the mainland coast. I misguidedly believed that this was a soft option as it included food and accommodation, but I soon discovered why this wasn't a popular choice with travellers. The accommodation was abysmal, rife with cockroaches; and the work entailed several hours a day of unblocking stinking toilets. The clientele was largely American,

Working as a maid in Greece

and although there were clear signs in English that toilet paper should be put into the bins rather than in the toilets, this concept was apparently too much for them to grasp.

With my dark hair and olive skin, wearing the same uniform as dozens of Greek maids, I became invisible to the hotel guests. I spent hours every day mopping the huge hall floors, listening to the American tourists discuss their holiday, how crap the food was, and what had happened the night before in the disco. Sometimes the male-only conversations included comments about the maids, including myself, as they assumed I was one of the locals who spoke no English – a source of great amusement to me. They might have wondered why I was smiling to myself as I mopped away.

For three months I unblocked toilets and polished floors, blending in with the furniture and letting go of my natural inclination to stand out. I found myself, for the first time since my youthful underwater experiences, in a meditative state. It was my first experience of mindfulness, although the word was not yet in my vocabulary. With no need to interact with anyone I could access a place of stillness inside. "Chop wood, carry water" say the Zen monks. Even the task of excrement disposal can be a doorway into consciousness when you are mindful of each action, and present in every moment.

In the wild flowers in the kibbutz, age nineteen

CHAPTER 5
Land of the Midnight Sun

After three months in the cockroach-infested digs of the Golden Coast Hotel, I had saved enough money to get to my next port of call. I'd decided to re-join Gary who was living in Olympia, the capital of Washington State on the west coast of the U.S. The town sounded like a cool hippy hangout and I was ready for a change of scene.

Olympia was indeed an interesting place to live; the first large vegetarian, buckwheat-chewing, bread-making community I had encountered. Gary and I were renting the cheapest accommodation available, a dingy bedsit, which I cheered up with plants I dug up in the forest and planted in coffee tins. Despite my best efforts to make the most of my life there, I very quickly felt like I was marking time; adrift with no purpose. The only jobs available without a green card were minimum-wage motel cleaning and waitressing – uninspiring to say the least. On top of which, my relationship with Gary was turning into a horrible, passionless compromise. It was like being a prematurely old, married couple locked into a pointless domestic routine.

Periodically, I would escape to travel with friends who came over to visit. On one occasion, I hiked down the Oregon and Californian coast with Lindsey and her American boyfriend from the kibbutz; and on another through Arizona and the Grand Canyon with my friend Rosy. The inevitable return to Gary and the apartment when money ran out started to fill me with dread.

We had a respite from Olympia one apple-picking season when we travelled up to Tacoma, intent on making our fortune in the apple orchards. In comparison with the Mexican immigrants who flocked up there every year and worked like Trojans, we were pretty pathetic. There's more to being a successful apple picker than meets the eye.

The first week or two were spent learning the skill of throwing the ladder into a tree correctly, positioning each throw for the maximum yield and getting every single apple off the tree. Then there was the art of twisting the apple so as to remove the stalk from the tree, but not the leaves, while holding the fruit gently to avoid bruising. I took on the task with a fighting spirit and copied everything my fellow workers did, eventually getting fit enough to run up and down the ladder at full speed. By the end of the season I was earning fifty dollars a day – a fortune compared with my motel jobs – and I returned to Olympia well pleased with myself.

Back from Tacoma with extra cash in my pocket I grabbed the opportunity to leave the US. I bought a ticket to London, intent on trying my hand at being an *au pair* in a nice English family – but I had underestimated how expensive London was, and how overcrowded the job market. Having arrived at Heathrow with only fifty pounds in my pocket and no friends or connections, in three short days I found myself penniless, homeless and jobless.

Out of ideas, in a tragic up-yours gesture to the universe, I walked into a pub and used my last pound to drown my sorrows in a pint of cider. A friendly Aussie sat beside me at the bar, noticing the tears trickling down my cheeks, asked me what was up. After listening to my tale of woe, he came up with a novel but intriguing suggestion – to contact an Icelandic company that apparently "imported" healthy young foreign girls for their fish processing season, which had just begun. This chap's girlfriend had recently left for a five-month stint in a fish factory, expecting to earn a great deal of money – which is how he knew the ins and outs of the deal.

The proposition sounded perfect for my predicament, particularly as employee flights, accommodation and food were all paid during the contract period. The cherry on the top was the fact that this company favoured South African, Aussie and Kiwi girls because they were considered hardier than other cultures, and less likely to renege on the contract.

My new Aussie friend, truly an angel in disguise, walked me to a phone booth, offering to pay for the phone call. I was informed that the quota of foreign workers had been full – but that, as fate would have it, one of the girls had taken ill and been flown home, freeing up a place especially for yours truly! Within hours of the health check and contract signing, I was on a flight to Reykjavik, the capital of Iceland, and on from there in a jeep to Faskrudsfjordur, a tiny village on the east coast of the island. I arrived in the land of the midnight sun in mid-winter, when it was dark for twenty-two hours out of twenty-four, and snow storms raged outside our windows for a large part of the day. I didn't mind at all. I felt liberated for the first time since leaving South Africa.

I made friends easily enough with the other girls, sharing rooms in the "slaughter house" – a building previously used for killing sheep, but refurbished quite pleasantly for our stay. Away from everyone I knew, I took on a new identity, calling myself by my middle name, Eva. Along with the new name, I found myself experimenting with adopting a different personality. After my claustrophobic domestic existence in Olympia I was bursting at the seams and I became the wild one in the group, regularly getting drunk and dancing like a crazy woman in the snow.

In the factory I was positioned opposite a lovely middle-aged woman called Innes who smiled encouragingly at me as she showed me the ropes; skinning and filleting cod and haddock off the bone, wasting as little as possible. Rather than being smelly, everything in the factory was kept spotless, with water flowing continuously over the illuminated perspex tables at which we were stationed. Factory work was paid on a bonus system where the more fish you processed and the less you wasted, the more you earned. Within a month I could slap those fishies on the table and slice them into pretty fillets faster than Bruce Lee chops bricks. I was accumulating a pleasing amount of money in the bank account they set up for me; feeling prosperous and free.

We made our own entertainment outside of the factory – playing cards, listening to music and getting legless on the weekends in true Scandinavian tradition. There were two phases to the week. Phase one: keep your head down and work your arse off, preferably doing overtime so as to earn as much as possible. Phase two: dress up on Friday night and meet up with the gang, which included anyone standing between the age of thirteen and forty. We would then cruise around the village's one circular road in old Cadillacs, *Grease*-style, gradually drinking ourselves into oblivion. This may not sound like your idea of a great night out, but you had to be there! Sunday was spent recovering in order to enter phase one again, bright and early on Monday morning.

We drank Iceland's most famous (and also cheapest) alcohol, Brennivin, a caraway-flavoured Schnapps. The custom was to mix it in a fifty-fifty ratio with Coca Cola in the small old-fashioned glass bottles. Strangely, no one ever drank the first half of the bottle – we simply poured it out the car windows, so that the sidewalks were dotted with brown piss-holes in the snow. Sometimes there were special activities on Friday night; a party in another village or, when the weather started warming up, a fire on the beach. The drinking, however, never varied. You stopped only when you passed out, usually sometime on Saturday morning.

One Friday night after imbibing a man-sized dose of Brennivin, I went home with a cute young boy Pieter to what I assumed was his flat. I woke up on the Saturday morning hung-over and disoriented, to find the lady who worked opposite me in the factory grinning over me. To my horror I discovered that Pieter was Innes' grandson, and only thirteen years of age! Almost more disconcerting was her total lack of shock or disapproval at finding me in her grandson's bed. She bustled around organising breakfast, for all the world as if I was an invited guest about whom she'd forgotten. Such were the ways in this part of the world; there were simply not the same taboos around the subject of sex to which I was accustomed. I remembered back to the Scandinavian girls on the kibbutz and understood their behaviour much better in the light of my Icelandic sojourn.

As the days lengthened, the snow storms abated and dozens of icy waterfalls and rivers streamed down the green mountains of the fiord. All of the other girls left when their five-month contracts were complete, but I stayed on for a further two months, plotting my next move. I went for long walks on my own, reflecting on my journey and my desires for the future. My time in Iceland was drawing to a natural close and I had no desire to return to Olympia.

Flush with cash for the first time since I'd started travelling, I planned a voyage to more tropical climes, settling on Hawaii as a suitable first destination. I needed to dry out after my excesses in Iceland; to nurture my body and reconnect with the sun and the ocean. I indulged in a glorious shopping spree, kitting myself out for some serious camping on the beach; a new down sleeping bag, igloo-frame tent, camp bed and gas stove included. I also splashed out on an expensive new camera, something for which I'd been longing since I'd left home.

I touched in with Gary back on the mainland, made my excuses and set off for the islands with a tentative plan to stay for a few months before moving on to travel the East. My relationship with Gary had evolved into more of a platonic friendship than a romance, but I nevertheless had a nagging suspicion that I was stringing him along. I liked the security of someone waiting back home for me while I adventured the globe, working out where – or indeed who – I wanted to be.

Hiking through the Grand Canyon in the snow

Picking apples in Tacoma

Picnic in the land of the midnight sun

With three of my factory co-workers

Working in the factory (me on the left)

My home, the slaughter house

CHAPTER 6

Wake-up Call in Paradise

My journey to Hawaii commenced with a Hare Krishna encounter at the airport – one where you think you're being given a book, and once you've accepted it's too embarrassing not to pay the five dollars that are belatedly requested. Actually, I *was* interested in the philosophy of the shaven-haired, orange-robed tribe, and I *did* need some reading material, so I didn't mind. It might after all take me one step closer in my quest for the meaning of existence.

I chose Kauai as a starting point; a relatively small and un-touristy isle with stunning mountains and beaches. My first discovery on landing, however, cast a gloomy outlook on my plan to camp long-term on a quiet beach. Local law specified that visitors were allowed to stay only three nights at any particular campsite. As I'm the kind of camper who takes all day setting up – making my tent into a palace and practically planting a garden outside – moving every three days was *not* an option.

The universe responded in a magical way to my dilemma. Hiking across to the island's south coast on my first day, I was picked up by a hugely hairy and wonderful hippy. Hearing my predicament, he offered to put me up for a couple of nights in his self-built wooden tree house, constructed on stilts in the middle of a beautiful forest. How could I resist?

Bill was the first true eco warrior I'd encountered on my travels. Climbing up the rope ladder to meet his girlfriend and their two-year-old daughter was like stepping into *The Jungle Book*. They lived without power or running water, up in the treetops; eating vegan, fetching water from a stream and cooking over a hand-made wood burning stove. They rose with the dawn and retired with the setting sun. These people lived as one with their environment and seemed to be as much a part of the forest as the birds and the trees.

Thus it was, through the lovely eco-hippy family, that I came to learn about Secret Beach. When I had first voiced my desire to camp out for a month or two, Bill had hinted that he might be able to help me. During the two days and nights I spent with him in the forest I could sense him checking me out. He loved his island, and he wasn't going to give out its secrets to anyone who didn't respect the land. I must have passed muster.

Secret Beach, Kaui

On the third day Bill dropped me and my backpack at the side of the road above Secret Beach. I had sworn a solemn promise to keep my knowledge of the beach to myself and also to leave no trace when I moved on. Known only to the locals, this beach was completely tourist-free, largely due to the fact that the path leading down to it was a steep and slippery cliff face. The fact that this was not a registered beach also made it free from legislation, which meant that I could camp there indefinitely!

As I negotiated my way down the muddy mountainside, tottering under the weight of my backpack, I understood why it was not so popular. But oh my Goddess was the slide and the muddy bum worth it! The sand stretched out in a stunning white expanse, backed by the luscious green hillside dotted with tropical trees. A little fresh water stream trickled through the lower hillside, and a grassy green ledge about twelve feet above the high tide level looked like it was made for my new tent.

For two weeks I was in heaven. The only non-insect or bird being I saw on the beach was a lone man who jogged down the beach occasionally, saluting me with a smile as he passed by. I had enough basic food supplies to last me for a few weeks, supplemented by coconuts and bananas from the land. If rejuvenating in nature was what the doctor had ordered, I'd found the perfect prescription and self-made spa resort. The hypnotic sound of the waves lulled me into a state of no-man's land – a neutral zone, where I let go of my planning and anxiety about the future. I walked on the beach, read and slept, thankful to have this opportunity to recover from the grind of the fish factory and my over-indulgence in Icelandic alcohol.

It was winter in Hawaii, which meant that although the days were sunny and gorgeous, the water was too rough for swimming. I had been warned by Bill that the undertow was vicious at this time of the year. To illustrate his point, he'd said that a coconut which fell into the water on this coastline would be sucked out to Hong Kong in a matter of days. I wasn't about to test the theory. Or so I believed.

One night, cosy in my tent with my home-made candle and foil lamp, I picked up the Hare Krishna book. I'd been postponing reading it since it had been placed in my hands, strangely anxious about what I might encounter in its pages. Once I started the book, however, I was hooked.

Absorbed in the intriguing new concept of reincarnation, I was subliminally aware of the wind growing stronger around me. Late into the night when the flapping of my tent blew the candle out, I finally put the book down and succumbed to sleep. My last thoughts were afflicted by the fear that at my present level of consciousness, I was sure to be reborn a dog. The increasingly loud sounds of an approaching storm whipping the sea into a fury only added to my unease.

When a storm is predicted in Hawaii, officials in helicopters use megaphones to warn campers to move to higher ground. Secret Beach was not, however, on the official listing of beaches. I had imagined that camping twelve feet above the high tide level was totally safe – I had no idea that winter storms could produce towering thirty foot waves that uprooted houses in their wake.

In the early hours of that morning a massive, thundering wave picked me up in its arms – sleeping bag, tent and all. It tossed me backwards into the icy embrace of the Pacific Ocean as effortlessly as a giant throwing a tennis ball. Or a coconut … remember the coconut that could get sucked out to Hong Kong in a matter of days? That was me – a round ball of waterproof nylon, somersaulting across the sea with my belongings crashing around me like a bag of marbles in a washing machine.

Three thoughts exploded in my brain in quick succession: (1) I'm going to be reborn a dog (the reincarnation thing). (2) I don't want to end up dead in Japan (the coconut thing). (3) I have to get out of this tent!

There was no time to contemplate my impending death – I had to snap into gear. As I managed to tear a gash in the nylon, a stream of icy water slapped me in the face and started filling the tent. I ripped harder, desperate to escape a watery grave, eventually fighting my way out into the freezing ocean. When my shoulder bashed painfully against something large and solid, my first instinct was to grab it with both arms, hoping that it might be a floating log. In a sea that wild, I knew I had no chance of staying above water for long without something to hold onto.

Miraculously, I felt the vicious wave draw away from my body, and realised that I was hanging onto the branch of a tree rooted into solid ground! The beach and my camping ledge were completely submerged under the rising water, and I'd been thrown back at the cliff straight onto a tree. Frantically I pulled my frozen body higher up the slope, out of reach of the terrifying waves.

And there I was, dressed only in a t-shirt and knickers, caked in mud from head to toe. I huddled in a shivering ball at the foot of a clump of trees, waiting for my brain to defrost enough for the practicalities of the situation to dawn on me. My mind was functioning in bite-sized pieces. I was alive. I'd been given another chance to avoid the rebirth-as-a-dog option, for which I was genuinely grateful. I was shivering uncontrollably and I had no other clothes.

The immediate solution that presented itself was to tear some large banana leaves off and wrap them around myself, snuggling into the undergrowth where I was protected from the wind. Over the course of the next few hours, waiting for the dawn and listening to the wind gradually abating, a list of what the ocean had just swallowed catalogued itself in my mind. My tent, my sleeping bag, my backpack, my passport, my traveller's cheques, my clothes – it was a duplicate of the very list of necessities I'd drawn up only a few weeks before my Hawaii trip. My mind couldn't take in what had just happened. I lay there in the gathering light in a state of shock, the rising sun gradually thawing my bones.

My emotions kicked in when I thought about my new camera sinking into oblivion. A wave of despair engulfed me and I sobbed hopelessly into my arms. I'd taken a series of unbelievable rainbow shots since I'd arrived on the island, and it crushed me to think I would never see them. My tears were not so much for the loss of the camera, but for the creative outlet I was discovering through my camera lens. Capturing the beauty of nature on film had been helping me to see the world through new eyes.

I hiked into town wrapped in a banana leaf skirt, my long hair in muddy dreadlocks. The islander who picked me up didn't seem surprised by my story – I was just another tourist caught out in a storm. On the way to the capital town of Lihue, he kindly stopped by his house in order to give me some old flip-flops and baggy jeans. I received a similarly casual reception at the police station where I reported my lost belongings and travellers cheques. Still in a state of shock, I made a return-charge call to Gary. When he insisted on buying me a ticket for the next flight back to Seattle, I was too dazed to resist.

In the aftermath of my brush with death I questioned the point of continuing my travels. What had been the purpose of going to Hawaii? To avoid resolving my relationship with Gary, and to recover from the hard work and hard drinking in Iceland. What had I been doing in Iceland, apart from the fact that it racked up points on my been-there-done-that list? Saving money in order to travel. Most of that hard-earned money had just been digested by the Pacific Ocean. It was time to go home.

Gary took the news of my decision to return to South Africa with a sigh of resignation. On a conscious level he wanted me to stay – but on a deeper level he knew that the relationship had been over for some time. He was free to start again, released from the river of our journey together into an ocean of new possibilities.

The Hare Krishna book taught me about life after death, and that the purpose of every incarnation is to learn and evolve. The synchronicity of this opening, on the very same night that I stared death in the face, was a wake-up call I couldn't ignore. It was time to engage in the game of life and make something of it! No more marking time, no more avoiding responsibility. On the plane, Bob Dylan crooned plaintively in my head:

> You better start swimmin'
> Or you'll sink like a stone
> For the times, they are a-cha-anging

PART 2
Saturn Return

CHAPTER 7
Facing the Lion's Den

My flight to South Africa included the option of a free stopover in Portugal. I decided to take advantage of the offer and have two weeks' time-out in Porto to assimilate my break-up with Gary, and simultaneously brace myself for *the big return*. While I was in limbo I also elected to go on a starvation diet – this being my preferred method of weight loss in my twenties. It seemed important to arrive home looking good after my three-year absence.

My novel self-styled Portuguese diet consisted of a couple of plums during the day, with the odd glass of port thrown in – it would have been remiss to be in Porto without indulging in a few port-tasting tours. Then, in the evening, I'd have a half bottle of red wine with some olives, sitting on the banks of the river Porto. My only interaction with people was an occasional chat in Pidgin English with the children who played on the water's edge. While the other tourists sat in smart little restaurants along the waterfront, I dangled my bare feet in the river, drinking my wine straight from the bottle like a hobo.

I fancied myself a romantic, artistic figure – much like the deluded character Art in the series *My Life in Film*. The meaning-of-life-and-death thoughts that had been born in the icy waters of Secret Beach rattled around in my brain. It seemed that the universe had conspired to get me back home, but further than that I couldn't figure out what I was supposed to do.

Two weeks later, having lost three kilos and turned the ripe old age of twenty-three, I boarded the plane back to South Africa. It was my fourth birthday since leaving home, having turned twenty in Israel, twenty-one in the States and twenty-two in Iceland. In my imaginary *Life in Film* episode that was significant.

In my absence, my parents had relocated from our family home to a small townhouse in an area of Johannesburg completely unfamiliar to me. It felt very strange driving into the anonymous,

security fenced-in compound where they now lived. Even more
disconcerting was the discovery that my old Zulu friend Katy was no
longer in my parents' employ, having retired to her tribal homeland. I
had not had a chance to say goodbye to her, and I never saw her again.
My roots had been displaced and there was very little which felt like
coming home.

The excitement of my home-coming on the part of my family
and friends was short-lived. Everyone was wrapped up in his or her
own drama, and my tales of exotic adventures in distant places only
lasted a dinner party or two. As I'd feared all along, my return to
South Africa meant only one thing – I was going to have to decide
what to do with my life!

Choosing a career is usually equated with deciding "what you
want to do" – but when you finish your studies, what you generally
want to do is lie on the beach with a glass of wine, watching the sun go
down. Or you might want to do something creative or humanitarian
that society considers impractical as far as earning a living goes. In
Western society the buzz words around employment choices are *duty,
responsibility* and *money*. In my case, I was torn between my desire to
please my parents and the inner voice urging me to do something
meaningful and enjoyable.

Teaching was the first option I considered; a vocation towards
which my B.A. degree could actually contribute. I knew that I could
teach – I'd known that all the way through my junior and senior
schooling. I remembered squirming with frustration when a teacher
failed to get a concept across effectively, wanting to stand up and
take over the lesson right there and then. I found myself tutoring
classmates before exams; breaking complex subjects down into bite-
sized pieces to make them easier to grasp.

I hadn't, however, come across any teaching opportunities
outside of the school system – and the prospect of being a school
teacher didn't thrill me. I loathed the idea of marking homework
and staff meetings, not to mention fitting in with the uptight South
African education system. Pursuing a career as a teacher also meant
going back to uni to do a teacher's diploma – an option that felt like a

backward step after so many years of freedom.

I was staying with my parents for the first time since I'd left for university at seventeen, and I hated being trapped in suburbia. The incessant background noise of the television news drove me nuts – I needed to earn enough money to move into my own digs as soon as possible. As I went through the newspaper ads I was lured by the scent of money, which was synonymous with independence. I spotted an IBM trainee programmer position, blagged my way through the interview and started work immediately. Computers were the big new thing, the pay was great, and my parents were over the moon that I was finally getting "a real job."

I was excited to be living in a big city with money to throw around for a change. I moved into a shared house, spent money on clothes and replaced my Brennivin and Coke habit with the more sophisticated and trendy Tequila Sunrises. Johannesburg had woken up to the underground party scene, and warehouses had been converted into psychedelic clubs that were a massive upgrade from the discos of my teen years. In the new clubbing scene it was totally acceptable to go partying on your own, which I loved.

Punk was still a big influence in South Africa in the eighties and I often pogoed into the early hours. There were many mornings when I crawled into work after a few hours' sleep, scratchy-eyed, yawning my day away in the self-study unit. My plan to become a programmer was flawed from the start by one very obvious factor – I had absolutely no interest in technology, computers or the business world. Six months into my apprenticeship I was called into the boss's office and unceremoniously given the boot.

Scuttling to hide my shame over my first failed attempt to sustain a proper job, I dived straight into a new endeavour – training as a cordon bleu chef. I loved cooking for friends, had a natural flair, and fancied myself as a private caterer. This was surely a move in the right direction – doing something that I enjoyed, and that had great potential as a self-employment option. This last, with the greater autonomy it offered, was becoming increasingly attractive to me.

However, as I progressed through the course, I was turned

off by the overly rich and fussy recipes, plus the prioritisation of
the appearance above the nutritive value of the food. Cucumbers
were blanched before using in case they caused an embarrassing
belch from a guest at your dinner party. Gravy for roasts was made
from a strained stock instead of from the flavours of the roasting
pan. Potatoes were shaved into perfect balls, wasting half of the
vegetable, not to mention all the nutrients under the skin. It was a
system of cooking that made no sense and which left zero room for
creative improvisation. Vocation lesson number two: when choosing
a profession, make sure you're selecting the right training! The rigid
cordon bleu style was simply not a good match for me. I passed the
program with flying colours, but by the end of the course I had lost
all desire to cook for a living.

Failing for the second time in the career department precipitated
an irresistible urge to run away from South Africa again. Of the
various cities I had visited in my travels, the one which most called me
to return was San Francisco. I wanted to live in an English-speaking
country, and I was sure I could find a better job this time round. To
fund this trip, I found a hostess position at the Top of the Carlton,
at that time the smartest tourist hotel in Johannesburg. The huge tips
from tables of drunken businessmen meant that in only three months
I had saved enough money to make my escape!

San Francisco was a welcome change on a cultural level. I
moved into a shared house with a serious young German student,
a depressed French lesbian and a large black American woman who
utterly fascinated me. Claudine cooked topless in the kitchen, her huge
bosoms attracting splats of batter as she flipped pancakes, singing
Grace Jones songs in a stupendous soprano. She was bisexual and had
a small bevy of consorts, male and female, whom she locked into her
silk-festooned boudoir when it pleased her.

My social life revolved around cappuccinos in a funky coffee
shop where I befriended a crowd of gay guys who liked my style.
They were serious posers who reignited my passion for taking arty
black and white photos. My work prospects, however, were decidedly
less glamorous than my home and social life. Without a green card the

best job I could find was in a screen-printing warehouse, robotically turning out hundreds of printed t-shirts every day. My fellow screen-printers got through the monotonous day in a haze of grass smoke, but I had to grin and bear it sober – there was no way I could maintain the coordination necessary to do the job while stoned! When my tourist visa ran out after six months, I accepted defeat and returned to Johannesburg.

It was crunch time. I felt like I'd messed up so much over the past few years that I simply *had* to find something worthwhile to do, and stick to it. I couldn't yo-yo back and forth from South Africa for the rest of my life, chasing rainbows in search of the illusive pot of gold. I rethought the idea of doing a teaching diploma. I knew that I was capable of teaching; there was no question about that. Could my misgivings simply be laziness, avoidance of hard work, or an unrealistic expectation of what life had to offer? It was time to find out.

Posing in San Francisco

CHAPTER 8

Cave Woman Gets Her Man

By March 1985 I was fully immersed in my teaching diploma course. I was working in a groovy late night jazz club to fund my studies – my most agreeable waitressing experience to date. The South African government had enforced an 11 p.m. public drinking curfew and Rumours was one of the many illegal clubs that sprang up to serve the after-hours crowd. The bar, fashionably stripped back, served only Irish coffees, tequila sunrises and straight scotch. I loved the eclectic bunch of regulars, and the fact that between 1 a.m. and closing the bar staff were officially allowed to drink with the customers.

One night a new Scottish barman turned up, and I fancied him instantly. The fact that Jeremy wasn't South African was the first factor that awarded him a high status in my books. Secondly, he was very cool behind the bar, in a Tom Cruise kind of way. He could take orders from several waitresses and pour the drinks, while simultaneously telling jokes to the customers. A born entertainer, he would juggle anything he could put his hands on when there was a lull in orders, perhaps combining a coffee cup, a lemon and a dinner plate – no mean feat in a confined space. He was also the only person I'd met who looked sexy talking with a cigarette dangling from his lips. There was something Clint Eastwood about it.

Aside from his smooth barman skills, Jeremy had a very endearing personality. I had been seeing an intense, intellectual Greek guy who didn't get on with anyone. Jeremy was the absolute opposite – sociable, funny, kind and open. Every ounce of my being shouted that this was the man for me, but he seemed oblivious to my feelings.

I hatched a plan to see Jeremy outside of working hours, joining the other staff members when they made a plan to see a popular jazz singer. On the big night I managed to secure the seat next to him and we chatted and joked, getting to know each other. A few hours and several tequilas later, I threw caution to the wind. He turned my way to say something, and I dove straight in for a snog. After a shocked pause, he returned my embrace. It was love at first kiss.

I hadn't planned on such a direct approach, but an animal instinct took over that night and made me pounce! A friend, who had decided on my behalf that things were moving too fast, separated Jeremy and I at closing time. She literally pushed Jeremy out of my doorway after I'd invited him into my flat for a coffee. After two days of torture in which I agonised over my inappropriate forwardness, a ray of sunshine arrived through my letterbox. A note written on a Rumours waitress pad contained Jeremy's invitation to "breakfast, lunch or dinner – or possibly all three" over the Easter weekend.

Two weeks into our relationship, once again under the influence, I asked him to marry me. That was when I discovered, to my horror, that he was only twenty-two! I was twenty-seven and had assumed he was at least as old as me. He had a confidence and worldliness about him that was absent in South African men of his age – and on a more superficial level, his slightly receding hairline made him look older than his years. In Jeremy's diplomatic way he managed to decline the offer without leaving me rejected, and for the meantime my drunken proposal was forgotten.

I realised I'd have to hang in there for a while, considering the age difference between us. I was experiencing my astrological "Saturn Return" which hits the first time round in one's late twenties. My mental state fitted in perfectly with the theory of what this return implies – a compulsion to think about one's future in terms of a career, children, partner, and a stable home. I was already keen to have children, but Jeremy wasn't even close to that kind of commitment.

In our first fifteen months together we were inseparable and blissfully happy. I cherished being with a man who was so loving, lovable, fun, spontaneous and supportive. But our bubble was burst unexpectedly when his father fell seriously ill, necessitating Jeremy's immediate return to Scotland. I had always known that he would go back to the UK, and had hoped that I would accompany him when the time came. The timing wasn't right, however, and we agreed that he should go it alone and spend as much time as was needed with his family. I was six months into my first teaching job, and knew that I would have a better chance of getting an overseas post if I completed the school year. After seeing his father through his illness, Jeremy's plan was to look for work in London, where we were to reunite for the Christmas of '86.

My year of teacher training had been a real strain. Being at uni in Jo'burg, this time as a mature student, was a completely different ball-game to my years in Cape Town. It was like being an over-sized school child again, suffocated by condescending teachers, trying to fit in despite my natural instinct to be a system-buster. As the training came to an end, I wracked my brain for a way to make my new career more stimulating and meaningful. The perfect opportunity presented itself in the form of an appeal for qualified teachers in Soweto.

Soweto, home for many years to Nelson Mandela, is a massive shanty town south-west of Johannesburg. An offshoot of the Apartheid regime, the township developed as thousands of indigenous people were forced to seek employment in the cities after their homelands were taken away. Temporary communities sprung up on the outskirts of Johannesburg, and as the years went by Soweto became an independent satellite town with schools, hospitals, hostels and sports stadiums.

In the mid-eighties, township music was coming to the forefront of the alternative music scene, and there was a certain amount of integration between the races in the poorer and artier areas of Johannesburg. Apartheid was collapsing organically, but segregation was still legally enforced. Everywhere you went there were still signs designating "White" and "Non-White" areas – separation of park benches, buses, restaurants, homes, schools and cities.

My incentives for wanting to teach in a township, however, were cultural rather than political. I wanted to get to know the original people of South Africa, who had been all but invisible to me in my childhood. The only black people I had known were Katy, our afore-mentioned maid; and Simon, the gardener employed by my mother. I applied for a post in a secondary school teaching English and geography and was accepted immediately. Most of the teachers at the school had neither a degree nor a teaching diploma, and the headmaster was thus thrilled to have me on-board.

The first assembly at Thomas Afolo School had me in tears. My memories of singing hymns at secondary school were of a hall of disinterested children struggling to stay in tune with one another. Here, several hundred children sounded like a choir of angels letting rip in a joyous heavenly celebration! Many of them swayed, danced unselfconsciously or clapped as they sang, and the teachers joined in with gusto. I was utterly perplexed by how one race of people could be so much more musically inclined than another.

It transpired that I was one of the first white teachers to work at the school, and the kids were openly curious about me. I loved their spontaneity and lack of inhibition; their physicality and cheekiness. In the classroom, however, I was faced with the challenge of preparing lessons from textbooks that were out of date, with little of the equipment which had been available in my training —slideshow and overhead projectors were unaffordable luxuries. I was also forced to acknowledge that no matter *where* I was teaching, I couldn't escape the dull necessities of the job – getting through the syllabus, setting exams, preparing and marking lessons.

My fondest memories of Soweto are not of the school, but of my daily drive along the pitted, dusty roads in the early morning sunlight. Women carrying bundles of wood on their heads and grandfathers smoking their pipes on doorsteps smiled at me as I passed. I envied the simplicity of their lives, despite their hardships. Like the school children I taught, they seemed so much more alive than the people of my privileged culture.

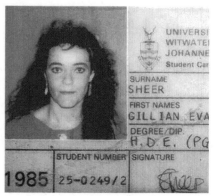

Waitressing at Rumours – the era of perms & berets

The shanty town of Soweto

Children skipping   Women carrying water

CHAPTER 9

Opening Doors

By November 1986 my move to London was imminent, and I was stressed to the nth degree. I found it difficult to admit, even to myself, how much I had struggled with my first year of teaching. It was too much to contemplate that my new career path might be a red herring after the past two years of hard work and dedication.

Another factor causing me anxiety was Jeremy's almost total lack of communication during our time apart. He had warned me that he was not good at correspondence, but it was hard to accept that we could be so intimate one moment, and so distant the next. Despite his assurance that he still wanted me to join him, I was increasingly nervous about my imminent emigration to the UK.

To take my mind off my worries, I decided to do a weekend massage course being led by my friend Vanessa. I'd never tried my hand at massage, or even experienced one, but I liked the idea of having some bodywork skills to use on friends. As the date of the workshop approached a feeling of excited anticipation arose in me, as if something of significance was about to unfold.

I arrived at the venue to find the massage tables assembled under huge Jacaranda trees on the rolling lawn of a fabulous garden. After we had all been shown the basic strokes, I lay down to receive a first practice session in leg effleurage. It felt wonderful to be massaged, lying outside on a warm summer day, a slight breeze wafting the scent of the fragrant flowers in the air around me. When it was my turn to have a go I remember thinking "Hey, I can do this, it's easy! What a great way this would be to earn money!"

It wasn't a professional course where the approach is often serious and clinical, causing the students to feel anxious about getting the techniques right. We were being taught basic massage skills such as effleurage and kneading, and then encouraged to tune into our partner's body and improvise. By the end of the weekend I was thoroughly enjoying my new skills and felt that I had real promise as a masseuse.

Vanessa knew that I was about to leave the country, and suggested that I give her a massage before I left. She said that receiving her feedback would consolidate the techniques I'd learned, and make it more likely that I would continue. The idea of giving my teacher a session was a bit nerve-wracking, but I realised that if I chickened out I'd be missing a valuable opportunity. We made a date for the following week and I steeled myself for what felt like a test.

Doing a full body massage for the first time and combining the various parts of the routine that we had practised was quite a challenge. Vanessa gave me equal doses of criticism and encouragement, and through her tutelage I corrected lots of potential bad habits. An exhausting hour-and-a-half later, I realised that that there was more to a good massage than meets the eye – and that I was possibly not as gifted as I had imagined.

Afterwards, during our chat over a cup of tea, Vanessa came out with something that totally took me by surprise. She said, "If you're stuck for a job in London, just blag your way into a massage job. You're a natural!" As much as I protested, she insisted that this was true – she believed that massage was an innate skill, and that I was someone who had a natural inclination for it. Much encouraged, I stored that fertile seed in the back of my mind.

There was another crucially significant event that took place in the weeks preceding my departure from Johannesburg. I would go so far as to say that it was my first true awakening experience. My dear friend Lindsey, knowing how anxious I was about my future, booked me an appointment with a woman named Agnes to "help me sort out my head." She assured me that the session was exactly what I needed to put things in perspective but, mysteriously, refused to tell me what Agnes actually did. I knew she had helped Lindsey's mum when she was struggling to cope with her husband's death, but that was all.

As it turned out, Agnes was a medium – a term which in any case would have meant nothing to me. Agnes' psychic skills were awesome – they allowed her access to my personality as well as to my past, present and future. She spoke of things both mystical and practical, including what the colours in my aura signified and the changes that were needed in my approach to life. She repeated several times that the key to my success in this lifetime was to "turn negative into positive." This, she said, would be something that I would teach others to do as well, and was the purpose of my present incarnation.

When Agnes spoke of times to come, she described my impending move "across the seas," which she assured me was set in the stars. She also saw a gold and ruby ring on my finger, which had belonged to another soul. The woman spirit in question came forward to give me her blessing for my future engagement – she was pleased that her ring would be used for a special new purpose. Agnes also saw contracts being signed, champagne glasses and two children, a boy and then a girl. A flood of joy and relief washed over me at this vision of my future. She was confirming that my union with Jeremy was meant to be!

Finally, she described other lifetimes I'd had on this planet; as a temple dancer in ancient Egypt and as a humble maiden at the time of Christ. When I'd read the Hare Krishna book, reincarnation was just a theory – it was amazing to hear Agnes describing *my* past lives, and to be told how they related to my present incarnation.

I felt an overwhelming love surround me as the messages were transmitted, and tears of gratitude rolled down my face. I knew in every atom of my being that what Agnes was saying was true. The purpose of the reading had been to reassure me that my move to London was positive, but in the process something far more important occurred. I learnt that I had a purpose in this lifetime, and that in the fulfilling of this purpose I would assist others.

And So It Is.

CHAPTER 10

Culture Shock

I hadn't anticipated how much of a shock my move to the UK was going to be. My outgoing personality crashed into the wall of British reserve, and for the first time in my life I found it difficult to make friends. I felt as though the people I met didn't like me, when in fact they were simply reserving judgement. South Africans are naturally welcoming to strangers, whereas the old-fashioned British approach is to hold back until they feel they can trust a newcomer.

Jeremy's family were terribly posh in comparison with mine, and their reservations about accepting me as a partner for the adored baby of the family were blatantly obvious. I was in a post-punk phase with an eighties Slade-type hair quiff and a largely fluoro wardrobe. It was impossible to tone myself down enough to feel that I fitted in.

My first meeting with the Colledge clan was in their family home in Scotland, a large country house grandly named "The Pavilion." Jeremy's mother was charm personified; elegant and sophisticated – I was simultaneously enchanted and intimidated by her. His father, very ill with cancer by the time I met him, was friendly but reserved. When he did have something to say, however, his dry wit and intelligence was apparent. By far the easiest family member to get on with was the younger daughter Catriona – nicknamed Tattie because of her love for potatoes, called "tatties" in Scotland. She had a subtle but wicked sense of humour and, like my middle sister Darrell, was the rebel of the Colledge family.

I had romantically envisaged my first Christmas with Jeremy sipping hot toddies in a pub around a fire, snowflakes falling on the windowpanes. The reality panned out as three consecutive days with the family at his elder sister Julie's elegant Clapham home, where I constantly felt like a fish out of water. I would dress up for one occasion only to find everyone looking super casual. At the following gathering I would dress down, and then be horribly embarrassed when everyone else was formally attired. I had the impression they actually liked to make me squirm as I sat at the dinner table, unable to contribute to their in-house conversations about family affairs or politics.

I was still in love with Jeremy, but things were very different from our free and easy time together in Johannesburg. Reunited with his family and old social circle, the conservative nature of his upbringing came to the fore. He remained the sweet, loveable person for whom I had fallen, but was going through a difficult period; enduring the very same pressures of career and responsibility that I had already faced. He was not enjoying his new city job as a trainee foreign exchange broker, and was drinking far too much – often entertaining clients late into the night.

At home in our crummy little Wandsworth flat while he was out drinking, I was desperately lonely and unsure if I would ever feel at home in this cold, grey city. I clung to Agnes' words of encouragement about my future, determined to make this new life work. I was *not* going to return to South Africa with my tail between my legs as I had after San Francisco.

Three months into my move, we were utterly broke. Without a work permit I was finding it impossible to get a job, and Jeremy's salary was hardly enough to keep us housed and fed. I remembered Vanessa's suggestion of talking my way into a massage job, and plucked up the courage to give it a try. Nervously, I set about phoning a list of health clubs in the Yellow Pages, prepared to lie about my qualifications. After only half an hour on the phone, I was invited to interview at a chiropractic clinic a block away from the famous Harley Street. Miraculously, I wasn't asked to present a certificate at the interview, but was simply asked to give the director a massage, following which I was employed on the spot!

The routine at the clinic was for patients to receive a half-hour back massage, followed by their chiropractic manipulation. Although I didn't earn much, it was an essential step in gaining experience as a bodyworker. It was also a huge confidence boost when I heard the regular clients, famous actors from the TV sitcom *'Allo 'Allo* included, asking for me in preference to the other therapists. Six months later when I finally secured a teaching post, I resolved to continue my massage practice from home as soon as I could afford to buy a table.

The post I'd been offered in North London was at an Orthodox Jewish school, where I taught the secular side of the syllabus – the other half of the children's day being dedicated to religious education. The focus at the school was mostly on Jewish studies, meaning that I had much more flexibility with the syllabus than at a conventional school. To put it another way, I got away with murder.

It was my first time teaching at a primary school level, and I was therefore required to cover all subjects on the curriculum: English, maths, science, biology, history, geography, art and physical education. My favourite activities with the children were those which stimulated their imagination and connected them with nature. Conversely, my pet hates were history and maths, and I felt bored stiff when I tried to teach from the prescribed textbooks. I found excuses to include art, storytelling and trips out into the playground under the most tenuous pretexts.

We would leave the classroom to find sticks to role-play a famous war, or to pick leaves for an art class which – according to my logbook – included some science or biology content. I loved the children, but the institutional aspects I'd disliked about my first teaching job were still very much present. I found it hard to relate to the other teachers and I was stifled by the paperwork, marking and endless rules-rules-rules.

It was time to let go of school teaching – and simultaneously time to let go of what anyone thought about that decision. Being a self-employed therapist offered a way to be totally independent and to do something I loved – which also involved helping people. Everyone around me warned against relinquishing my steady income. "Just do it part-time," they urged. That way, they said, I would always have my salary to fall back on when clients were thin on the ground. They pointed out that there were thousands of massage therapists in London, very few of whom made enough money to survive without a second job. I stubbornly ignored their warnings and plunged into my new career with unabated enthusiasm.

I bought my first massage table, enrolled on a reflexology course, and set about building up a client base through adverts in shop windows and local newspapers. Unfortunately, along with the genuine enquiries I received, I also had to deal with dodgy calls in which men inquired about "extras." I learnt in this way about the "massage parlours" that were a thinly veiled excuse for sexual services – and about the tainted reputation massage had acquired in these circles.

This would have been enough to deter most women therapists from working alone at home, but my determination to make a success of my new vocation was unwavering. I made my ad as transparent as it could possibly be, and laughed in the faces of any gentlemen who still made inappropriate suggestions. Within a few months I had built up a small base of regular clients, and was already earning more than I had as a full-time qualified teacher.

In my new role as a therapist I felt motivated and happy; I was finally doing something heart-centred that I truly enjoyed, and which didn't cramp my style to boot. But it wasn't only about the massage or reflexology – the words which flowed from me when I was working felt both inspired and inspiring. I was starting to experience the sense of purpose for which I had craved.

I was awakening spiritually, both through my healing work and through guidance I was receiving. I had started going to the College of Psychic Studies for a reading every four or five months – it had become my form of therapy, a kind of spiritual addiction. I was in awe of channels and mediums who had the ability to bring through information from an invisible plane of existence. What I loved in particular was the feeling of love and optimism that was invariably transmitted in the sessions.

I was always being told "Well done!" for little changes I'd made and hurdles I'd overcome. I was informed by one channel that I was often doing healing during a massage treatment without realising it, and this was subsequently confirmed by my clients. I was also told that my voice was a gift – that I could transmit healing codes through my voice that would ultimately assist hundreds of thousands of people. This was something which didn't make any sense to me at the time, but which proved many years later to be absolutely true.

I tended to go to for a reading when I had a burning question to ask, or when I was in crisis. When Jeremy's father Bill passed away, not long after my arrival in the UK, Jeremy descended into such a deep and dark depression that our relationship nearly fell apart. He withdrew into his pain and became distant and cold. Deeply unhappy, I went to see a medium whom I trusted implicitly. I didn't necessarily want to communicate with Bill – in fact, connecting with "loved ones who've passed over" was never my motivation for seeing a psychic. I simply wanted help from a higher perspective than my own. In this case, I wanted to know if Jeremy and I were still meant to be together.

When I had met Bill on our first trip to Scotland, I hadn't gotten to know him very well. In the session, however, I immediately recognised his personality – witty and understated – in the message that was transmitted. His most pressing purpose in communicating with me, he said, was to apologise for something he'd said to Jeremy shortly before he died!

He had apparently cautioned his youngest son about getting married too soon, a warning which he now feared was inappropriate. On his deathbed he had been reflecting on his other children's broken marriages and the heartbreak that had ensued in their wake – but from "the other side" he had a different perspective. He saw that our future marriage and children were not only destined, but were exactly what Jeremy needed – and that taking on these responsibilities was precisely what would assist him most in moving forward. He wished, in other words, to undo any doubts he'd planted in his son's mind about asking for my hand in marriage!

Bill asked me to pass this message onto his son, along with a firm instruction to stop wallowing in his own self-pity; redirecting his energy instead into supporting his grief-stricken mother. When I shared what I'd been told with Jeremy, he broke down in tears. Like me, he instantly recognised his father's energy in the messages, right down to the expression he had used to address him – "the boy." The advice from his father assisted him greatly in snapping out of his depression and getting on with his life.

It also saved our relationship in the nick of time, precipitating a much happier and more fulfilling phase for both of us. It would be a while before Jeremy proposed, but we were both committed to creating a life in London together. Things in rainy old London town were beginning to look up.

Post-Punk Gilly & Jeremy

On a barge trip

The Pavilion – Jeremy's family home

Early London days   Our first flat in Herne Hill (middle floor)

My London classroom

CHAPTER 11

You Can Heal Your Life

Jeremy's small but timely inheritance from his father enabled us to put down a deposit on our first property in London. After a year-and-a-half of renting a depressing shoebox, we were delighted to own a two-and-a-half bedroom flat in the up and coming suburb of Herne Hill. I loved stamping my mark on our cosy new abode, filling it with plants and decorating the rooms in the vibrant colours of my African homeland.

I was feeling decidedly more at home in England – settling in with Jeremy's family, making friends and loving my new work. We developed a penchant for the French game *boules,* in the process befriending the patrons of a cute little French restaurant not far from our home. We hung out with friends at Le Bouchon most weekends, eating *moules frites* and drinking Pastis on the pavement, continental style. The yearly Evening Standard Boules Competition in Battersea Park became the highlight of our social calendar. Jeremy's team, a Scottish trio called "Raging Boules" were in the finals twice – once accepting defeat to their French rivals; and the following year, triumph of all triumphs, claiming the trophy!

I was ecstatic when Jeremy finally asked for my hand in marriage, three years after my embarrassing drunken proposal. As predicted by Agnes, my engagement ring was antique gold, with a ruby at its heart. With gratitude, I remembered the blessing its first owner had given me. For the next six months I went into "Wedding Land," a realm all brides-to-be know well, in which my every waking moment was spent planning a fairy-tale wedding. We had chosen an elegant mansion house in Twickenham for the venue; however, were struggling with a budget that barely covered the hire cost, let alone anything else! Ever resourceful and determined, I found ways to economise in every direction, including getting a student designer from South Africa to make my wedding dress for the grand sum of fifty pounds.

To most conventional brides, my wedding morning would have been a nightmare. I was up at 4 a.m. in the Covent Garden market buying flowers for the reception, dispatching various friends to pick up boxes of wine and equipment, make the Pimms cocktails and do the floral arrangements. Despite my best efforts, the schedule went wildly awry, culminating in a scenario where I hadn't even made up my bride's bouquet or finished dressing by the time the wedding taxi drew up outside the flat! I literally threw some flowers together, raced outside with my high heels in my hand and did my makeup in the car. Unsurprisingly, I felt overwhelmed during the ceremony and found it hard to get my lines out through the tears that choked me. They were tears of joy, certainly; but also of relief that our big day was happening at last and there was nothing left for me to organise.

Thus it was that on the 24th of June 1989, a gloriously sunny day in the peak of the English summer, I became Mrs Gillian Colledge. The Twickenham house was the perfect choice for the reception, with its stunning English country garden and manicured lawns. As the Pimms flowed and we danced our first dance out on the grass I threw formality to the winds, discarding my formal high heels in favour of South African summer-style bare feet.

The highlight of the wedding was Jeremy's speech, in the form of a Karaoke-style song that he somehow managed to make tasteful. Ever the showman he had every man, woman and child in tears by the end. As we drove away in our wedding taxi, the assembled male guests lined up on the pavement outside, raising their kilts in the traditional bare-all send-off. Yes, Scotsmen really *do* go naked under their kilts!

After a short honeymoon in Crete we had a very special holiday with my parents. They were in London for the first time and we had promised to take them on a trip around Scotland while they were visiting. Having once been to the lochs of Scotland as part of a European tour, my mom had always dreamt of returning to the highlands. I was thrilled to be the one to make that dream a reality.

My parents loved Scotland's quaint B&B's, country hospitality and long summer days. There were two highlights on our journey for my dad, who was both a passionate golfer and fisherman – the first, a visit to the famous St Andrew's golf course and the second, a fishing excursion on the remote Isle of Skye.

Settling into married life in London, Jeremy and I were finally in a position to have the children for which I had always longed. When I fell pregnant a year into our marriage I was ecstatic. My jubilance, however, was short-lived – three months into my term I suffered a heart-breaking miscarriage. Having believed that the child I was carrying was the "Child of Light" many psychics had foreseen in my future, I was devastated. I went for a reading to ask for guidance on the loss of the baby and was advised that the cause of the miscarriage – the umbilical cord twisting around the baby's neck – had been unforeseen. I was assured that the same soul would return to me, and was urged to let go of anxiety and stay positive about any future pregnancies.

Within months I was pregnant again, this time thankfully carrying the baby full-term. We opted for a water-birth at home, ignoring the warnings from my doctor that a home birth was not a sensible option for the first birth of a woman over thirty after a miscarriage. At precisely 3:33 p.m. on the 15th of September 1991, our adorable baby Max emerged onto the Earth plane. Producing a whole new human being is surely the most incredible phenomenon in the world.

As happy as Jeremy and I were on every other level, money matters were often a source of tension between us. With our union and the new responsibilities of parenting and paying a mortgage, I entered an unchartered territory of bank loans, overdrafts and credit cards that made me extremely anxious. The universe heard my cry of despair and sent assistance my way in the form of an amazing book – *You Can Heal Your Life*, by Louise Hay. It was a book that turned my reality upside down – or right side up, depending on your perspective.

I have a strange habit of playing with books before I begin them in earnest – reading the back and front covers, skimming through the foreword and introduction, looking at the chapter headings, and sometimes dipping in here and there instead of starting at the beginning. This was no exception, and I couldn't resist commencing

with Louise's life story in the last chapter of the book. Her story
was the first I'd encountered in which a woman heals herself of an
"incurable" disease, in this case cancer, purely through changing
her thoughts and belief patterns. The fact is that the most powerful
spiritual teachers and leaders have often been awakened through
transcending a tragedy or illness.

As I finally read the first chapter, which includes a point-by-
point summary of Louise's philosophy, time stood still. I was receiving
a mighty revelation akin to the thunderous voice Moses heard beside
the burning bush. I read:

> We are each responsible for all of our experiences.
>
> Every thought we think is creating our future.
>
> The point of power is always in the present moment.

Up until then I had believed that stuff simply happened to me,
and that we were all victims of circumstance or fate. Sure, there was
free will, and I could choose to do things to try and improve my life.
Nonetheless, I had no idea that my *thoughts* had the power to create
my future. This was the first time I had come across the concept of
consciously manifesting or creating my reality.

The main tool Louise Hay proposed to set about transforming
your thoughts, and therefore your life, was the use of affirmations.
These are positive statements spoken in the first person, in the present
tense, as if you are already in the process of achieving your goals.
For example, if I'm having money troubles and I recognise that my
thoughts about money are less than healthy, useful affirmations might
be: "Money comes to me easily now. I let go of my fears around
money." Affirmations are designed to *reprogram* your limiting beliefs,
both conscious and unconscious. They only work if you are able to
trust that it is possible to change your life – and if you infuse your
practice with passion and conviction.

I believed and understood everything I read in the book, but
it wasn't an easy ride. The thoughts that needed an upgrade were
deeply rooted, and seemed to have a life of their own, racing around
my head all day and night. Nevertheless, my attitude towards our

financial situation was transformed almost overnight, simply through understanding that I could and would create abundance in my life, as my negative beliefs around money were reprogrammed.

The area of my life where I could most easily see that I *was* creating my reality in a positive way was in my work. Louise taught me that *I* was the one in charge of my life, and I could see how having belief in myself and following my heart had finally led me in the right direction. I loved the wonderful feedback from my massage and reflexology clients, and it suited me perfectly being my own boss.

It was so wonderful, after torturing myself for all those years about choosing the right career, to be on my path as a healer. And it had all begun with my choice to participate in Vanessa's massage weekend, "just for fun!" This is a basic Pleiadian concept in action – these star people teach and learn primarily through playing games and spontaneous experimentation. Even more remarkable was the realisation that, against all odds, my family and friends respected the profession I had chosen.

I was gradually getting the point of Earth life. It is a journey on which things only really flow when we are brave enough to follow our joy, and be true to ourselves.

My very Scottish wedding

My Dad, Jeremy and I on St Andrews
golf course

Max & I in the water-birth pool

'Raging Boules' with their French rivals

CHAPTER 12

Manifesting a Miracle

W hen Max was only nine months old, I noticed that six weeks had passed without my having had a period. Jeremy and I joked about the possibility of an immaculate conception – we were certain that we had not made love over that time interval. I was definitely not ready to have another child.

When a test proved that I was indeed pregnant and the doctor gave me the due date, I had a goose bump attack. The baby's birth date was identical to that of the child I'd miscarried two years previously! The shock of being pregnant again was tempered by my knowing that the very same soul who had chosen me as a mother had returned to my womb, this time to stay. Souls choose to incarnate on very specific dates because of the astrological implications. I accepted that Gabriella's conception, premature as it may have seemed to me, was in fact in divine timing.

With another child on the way we decided that it was time to sell our small flat and buy something bigger. This was a perfect opportunity to practice the new skills I had learnt from Louise Hay to manifest my dream house. I made a list of all the things I desired from our future home; including more space, a safe neighbourhood for the children, a lovely treatment room and a big garden. I also wanted to stay in South East London so that I could serve my existing clientele.

If money had been no problem, my mission might have been fairly easy to achieve. But when we told local estate agents our budget for a four-bedroom house with a large garden, they all but laughed in our faces. The first miracle occurred when we secured the promise of a one-hundred-percentage mortgage from the bank. We were selling our flat at a loss, having bought at the peak of the property boom in the eighties, and thus didn't have any cash for a deposit. The second miracle took a while longer to manifest.

For the first time I used visualisation as well as affirmations in my manifesting practice. I was guided to visualise not only the home I wanted, but also the people who would purchase our flat. I wrote and rewrote my list of affirmations, including one that read: "Our property is bought by a couple who will be very happy living here." As I said each sentence out loud, I pictured our new house with a large open-plan kitchen, a healing room with a view, vibrant colours everywhere and a garden filled with flowers and birds. The houses we viewed were so far from my dream, however, that I couldn't help wondering how much I'd be forced to compromise.

Months went by without our managing to either sell our flat or find an affordable house. I was starting to feel increasingly anxious about our lack of progress, but hung onto the belief that the affirmation-plus-visualisation process would produce results. Whenever I practised the technique, my faith that I really could manifest this dream was renewed. I could *feel* the energy of my imaginary home as if I was actually in it.

One thing that helped enormously was a psychic reading from my friend Lindsey Turner, in whose abilities I had absolute faith. She reassured me that there was a very good reason why we were being forced to wait for our new abode. She described our future home as having "a feeling of the countryside about it." She could see two children running around laughing in a big kitchen, a happy little terrier dog at their heels and French doors opening onto hollyhocks in the garden. It sounded wonderful!

At the very end of my pregnancy, a couple who were *identical* to the picture in my visualisations put an offer in for our flat. They were exactly as we had been five years before; about to be married, and just as excited about their first home together. The resemblance between the couple and the image I'd had of them was extraordinary.

As the transfer date for the flat loomed, we frantically put in offers for one house after another, determined to move before the baby was born – particularly as we'd planned a home birth once again. Apparently the time to buy was still not in the stars. Two weeks before my due date we were obliged to vacate our flat. Homeless and extremely stressed, we moved temporarily into a friend's council flat just up the road, on *Sunray Avenue*. She was broke, and it suited her to stay with her boyfriend for a couple of months while we paid her rent. My sweet baby girl, truly a ray of sunshine, was born there on the thirty-first of May 1993. Gabriella didn't mind living in limbo, but I was starting to lose the plot.

Looking at houses while Jeremy was at work with a two-week-old baby plus toddler Max in tow, I lost my perspective on what was acceptable. Over-tired and anxious, I couldn't see the wood for the trees. In this state, I took Jeremy to see a nineteen-thirties house in West Norwood which I'd viewed the previous day. I'd been attracted to its huge garden and low price, but the house itself was in a shabby state and I couldn't bear the idea of how much work was needed to make it liveable. It certainly wasn't my dream home – but something made me take Jeremy to view it before I wrote it off completely.

I remember Jeremy standing at the loft room window for what seemed like ages, staring at the panoramic view across London. He seemed oblivious of the long list of objections to the house that I was voicing. He lingered again at the bottom of the garden, hands on hips, with a big grin on his face. Afterwards he told me that in that spot, looking up at the house, his soul had announced that this was "his little piece of England."

For the previous two years he'd left it entirely in my hands to choose a property, because he knew how much time and passion I'd put into the manifestation of our new home. On that day, however, he came in from the garden and took the decision right out of my hands. He smiled at Mrs. Pipe, the sweet old lady who was reluctantly selling her beloved house, put his arm around my shoulder and declared, "This is it – this is our new home!"

We were the first people to view the house, and Mrs. Pipe liked our little family so much that she took it off the market immediately. Just as had occurred with the sale of our flat, the owner was reminded strongly of her own young family when they had bought the house. It was almost unheard of to sign on a property without going through a haggling process or having to compete with other buyers, but the universe said very clearly: "This is meant to be," and the sale went ahead effortlessly.

For a long time, I couldn't see that this was the house I'd worked so hard to manifest. I was too wrapped up in the grinding work of stripping wallpaper, painting, sanding floors and ripping up ugly brown carpets. The stress of playing mum and seeing clients whilst remodelling the house blurred my vision. The house was endlessly filled with dust as we forged ahead without professional builders, following a "plan as you build" approach. We were squeezing the pennies, but the claustrophobic proportions of the thirties design that I'd hated were gradually being transformed. As we made progress and the house took shape, it started to sink in that *every single thing on my wish list really was being fulfilled.*

We were in a cul-de-sac, a blessing that I hadn't fully cottoned onto when we first moved in. It made for a feeling of community – a wonderful change after our flat that had been on a busy main road. The local children played outside in the street, just as I had in my childhood, and I welcomed them into our garden to play with our little ones, the new favourite "pets" of the neighbourhood.

The view from all the back windows facing the garden was spectacular – and because there were no houses backing onto us, there was that feeling of space for which my African soul had been longing. My treatment room at the very top of the house was magical; up in the clouds overlooking the treetops, with the city of London in the distance. The whole vista changed colours along with the seasons and my clients loved being up there.

Years after that reading from Lindsey, when I'd long since forgotten the details, I came across the transcript and read it through again. It was fascinating to grasp how many of her predictions had come true. I finally understood one of the "very good reasons" why we'd had to wait so long for the house – because it hadn't been on the market until the very day I'd viewed it for the first time!

I laughed my head off when I read her depiction of the little terrier dog she'd foreseen as a part of our family. At the time of the reading I wasn't at all interested in getting a dog, and therefore hadn't paid any attention. We'd bought Wordie for the children when they were old enough to deal with a puppy, and her description of our family looking at a litter of tiny black puppies was uncannily accurate!

It truly was a home worth waiting for, as Lindsey's guides had said, and it did indeed have that spacious feeling of being in the countryside. Her description of the kitchen also fitted perfectly now that we had knocked down a couple of walls and built an adjacent wooden deck. But there was one detail in her portrayal of the house that didn't seem accurate – the French doors that she'd seen looking onto a garden with hollyhocks. Oh well, I thought, she was close enough.

Eleven years after moving into the house, when the children were too old to share a room and I was obliged give up the loft room, Jeremy built me an outdoor healing room. He more or less recreated our beach hut in Whitstable – a simple wooden structure with an insulated inside. The double glass doors looked out onto a garden filled with the flowers and birds, straight out of the visualisation I had done in my manifesting practice.

One day in my new sacred space I opened my eyes after a meditation and the penny fell into place – I was looking out of those exact French doors that Lindsey had described in her reading. My jaw dropped open as I realised that the flowers that had naturally seeded themselves right outside the room were hollyhocks! My home was a miracle, prophesied and manifested in perfect detail.

And the cherry on the top – something I hadn't even noticed when we bought the house – was our street address: *Portal Close!* This reference to the portal that was soon to open for me in this special house was a cosmic joke; the universe as always sending me a wink and smile as it aligned me with my destiny.

Max and Gabby aged three and one

Max in front of 15 Portal Close   Wordie as a puppy on the deck

Playing boules at the bottom of the garden with friends

PART 3
Reality Shift

Desperate Housewives

All through my twenties I daydreamed about what a perfect earth mother I would be to my beautiful, talented children. Patient and kind, I would encourage their creativity and connection with nature. Like most future parents I thought that I had deep insights into where other parents went wrong. Needless to say, the reality of motherhood came as somewhat of a shock!

Of course I loved my children passionately, but the overwhelming twenty-four-hour responsibility for these fragile and temperamental mini-me's felt like an assault on my freedom. After Max's birth, left alone all day while Jeremy worked long hours in the city, I felt anxious and overwhelmed. I was sliding into postnatal depression, but knew that I didn't need medication; I simply needed a helping hand. I put on my manifesting hat and created an affirmation for "a loving, competent, flexible and affordable child-minder, just around the corner."

Only days later, a neighbour gave me the number of a friend who had recently decided to look for childcare work; she loved babies, and her own children were grown-up. Brenda lived, literally, "just around the corner" from me! Our first meeting was hilarious – I was meant to be interviewing her, but it was so obvious that I was struggling with my two-week-old baby that it felt like it was the other way around. The minute she took Max into her arms to show me how to burp him, a wave of relief and gratitude washed over me. She was the wise, older sister or loving grandma that I lacked in London, and she saved my life. With her help three mornings a week, I was able to start seeing clients again. My equilibrium returned. I was an altogether better mother with some time-out to interact on an adult-only level, and use my healing gifts once again.

When we subsequently moved to our house and had a spare room, I employed our first live-in *au pair*, a lovely nineteen-year-old Polish girl, Lisa. "Au pairing" is a system which allows young foreigners to stay in a family home as a mother's assistant while they simultaneously attend language school and gain experience in the wider world. We had five different au pairs over the years, all Eastern European girls, fresh out of school and wide-eyed to be in the metropolis of London. I loved the injection of young-adult energy into the household, and this made me look forward to being a mother of teenagers. I befriended my au pairs, welcoming them into our home as one of the family, and in return they were a wonderful support for me as I settled into motherhood.

When the children were still toddlers, I went for a reading with a trance channel in North London whose guide was simply called The Master. Trance channels set aside their own consciousness to allow the guide to speak directly through them, and are therefore only subliminally aware of the material coming through. The Master spoke to me about the "Children of Light" – those now referred to as Indigo and Crystal. I learnt that these souls come from a higher level of existence than most of us, and are destined to be the new leaders of the world. I was told that Gabriella was a Child of Light and that her elder brother Max, although not as active spiritually, would support her on her journey.

I was also warned that these children can be difficult to mother, because they absolutely won't comply with anything that goes against their inner knowing. This guidance made me realise that Gabby's challenging attitude as a toddler was partly due to her frustration over the sometimes meaningless rules that were imposed upon her. I changed tack in my approach with the children and tried my very best to see them as wise light beings, giving them a sense of autonomy whenever I reasonably could. Jeremy was a more conservative parent than I, but we managed to find a happy middle ground, agreeing on boundaries that worked for us both.

Everything looked rosy in our little Portal Close world, but in the process of manifesting the life of my dreams, I slipped back into my old pattern of trying too hard, and needing to impress. Years later when I watched the TV series *Desperate Housewives*, I was tickled pink by the character of Bree Van de Kamp. She's a caricature of me as I was in those days; trying my best to be perfect in every way.

I channelled my creative talents into the house and garden, spending endless hours decorating: designing a country kitchen, an African living room and a sexy Parisian bedroom. I painted everything in sight – cushions, flowerpots, deckchairs and sofas. This was the first time I had my own garden, and I spent every spare moment digging flower beds, weeding, watering, and planting in different colour themes. For the children's birthday parties, I slaved over extravagant cakes shaped into cars, trains, Barbie dolls and castles, presenting myself in the image of the ideal mother.

The thing to do in our crowd was to "entertain" in the form of dinner parties, and I became the queen of entertaining. I would spend days planning the menu for a dinner, and the parties got bigger and more elaborate as the years went by. I remember hosting a Chinese-themed birthday party in which I served a seven-course Chinese banquet, transforming the dining room into an oriental palace just for the event.

Many years went by before I accepted that in trying so hard, my energy was flowing in a misplaced direction. I had manifested an idyllic suburban life and my work as a therapist was going well, but there was something missing. I felt an intense yearning to manifest the path of service that had been foreseen for me, and sent out a prayer for assistance – for something that would refocus me and lead me forward.

The response to my call was by far the most dramatic opening in my life – a doorway into the unseen realms that I had previously accessed only through the many psychics I had visited. My journey between worlds was set in motion, destined to change my life in the most joyful way imaginable.

Some of the over the top birthday cakes

Max's third birthday   Halloween at Portal Close

Max & Gabby with Lisa on the deck; hand-painted deckchairs & cushions

My English country garden

The family off to a christening - outside Portal Close

CHAPTER 14

Opening to Channel

Through the various readings that I had over the years, I encountered a multitude of guides with a higher, enlightened perspective on Earth life. This made me long for direct connection with my own guides, although I had no idea if this was possible. Like most people, I believed that one had to be born with a gift to be able to channel. When I first started going for readings I usually asked questions about the future, for instance about when we were going to find the right house or how many children I was destined to have. As I progressed on my path, however, my desire for spiritual guidance became stronger than my curiosity for what the future held.

I started to favour channels over those who called themselves mediums or psychics. Channels speak the words of their guides directly, instead of interpreting the images or messages they receive. In addition, their guides are usually higher dimensional beings, rather than the spirits of people who have passed over.

On a trip to Brighton in '97 I was strolling through a New Age shop, when a book literally fell off a shelf onto my feet. After perusing the pages briefly, I put it back – I was already halfway through several metaphysical books, and couldn't justify buying another. But when it fell off the shelf a second time, I realised that I really *did* need to pay attention to the sign I was being given. A feeling of excited anticipation arose in me as I walked out of the shop holding a book entitled: *Spiritual Growth: Being Your Higher Self*. It was one of the *Earth Life* trilogy transmitted through the American channel, Sanaya Roman.

Through Sanaya's wonderful guide, Orin, I was made aware that this particular time period in which we find ourselves is quite unique. As I sat on the train back to London, the opening lines of the introduction electrified me.

Greetings from Orin! You are entering a dramatic and exciting time. There is a wave of energy passing through your galaxy that is altering the course of all life it touches. This wave affects the very nature of energy and matter, bringing all matter into a higher vibration. You may be having more frequent psychic and telepathic experiences, and feeling a deeper need to know your life purpose and put it into action. You may feel you have less time and more to do, for this wave changes the nature of time. Some of us have come as guides to assist you during this special time.

I could actually *feel* Orin's powerful, loving energy transmitted through his words. I learnt more from him than any teacher I had yet encountered in the physical realm – information on how to lift the veils of illusion, connect with my Higher Self* and align with my highest purpose. Much to my delight, after overcoming his initial resistance to reading the book, Jeremy was as enthusiastic about the material as I was. We ordered the accompanying *Spiritual Growth* cassette tapes, which contained a series of guided meditations from Orin to reinforce the lessons from each chapter. For the first time, I felt that we were on a spiritual path together, as a couple.

Looking through the list of Sanaya's other books I came across one entitled *Opening to Channel*, co-written by her and Duane Packer. Even reading the title gave me goose bumps. This book taught me something that excited me beyond words – that *anyone* could communicate with their guides if they had the desire and the perseverance to practise. But on a practical level, the book didn't bring me any closer to making that leap.

I couldn't get past the simple exercise of visualising an image, for example a flower, for several minutes. The purpose was to focus your mind in order to cultivate the concentration necessary to channel. Visualisation didn't come naturally to me and my mind

---

* Your Higher Self is the aspect of your eternal soul which is with you in this incarnation. He/she knows your past, present and future, and constantly nudges you towards the experiences that will help you to evolve, and to remember who you are in the bigger picture, and what your purpose is. In some ways, you can consider your Higher Self to be your guardian angel, but he/she is also the true, wisest, YOU.

simply wouldn't stay focussed for more than a few seconds without wandering off in a dozen directions. This was incredibly frustrating, and made me doubt that I would ever be able to channel.

I didn't completely give up hope, however, and when we travelled to the west coast of the US for a family holiday in August '98, I packed *Opening to Channel* in my suitcase, with the intention of giving it another go. I also took a set of cassette tapes on channelling by Lita De Alberdi, who had trained with Sanaya. I had in mind that as we were visiting Mount Shasta, known to be one of the seven major chakras of the planet, I might be energetically assisted in making a connection with my guides.

In our starting point, San Diego, we rented a massive R.V. (recreational vehicle) and set off on an epic adventure through California and Oregon. Max and Gabby were respectively seven and five, and their movie of the moment was *Grease*, starring John Travolta. We spent long days on the road with Jeremy at the wheel – mountains, forests, beaches and hot springs whizzing by, the children and I playing the roles of Sandy and Danny to the tune of "Grease is the word, it's the time, it's the place, it's the action."

With three weeks to visit dozens of sites, we ended up scheduling only two days in Mount Shasta. The universe, however, conspired to keep us there long enough for the true purpose of our excursion to unfold. We arrived in the Shasta campsite early one

Mt Shasta & Lake

evening, in a beautiful forest adjacent to a transparent green lake, the snow-clad mountain painting a magnificent backdrop. Having chosen a lovely campsite deep in the forest, Jeremy painstakingly manoeuvred the huge vehicle back and forth until it was perfectly positioned, and switched off the engine. Just as we smiled at each other, relieved at having arrived after eight hours on the road, an alarming *CLUNK* echoed through the trees as a vital part of the engine dislocated.

On the phone to the rental company we were told that the only engineer qualified to fix the problem would have to travel all the way from San Diego. The operator regretfully informed us that it would be a minimum of four days before we were on the move again. Rather than feeling put out, we were both relieved to be coerced into staying stationary for a while. We were exhausted from the massive distances we had travelled, and could feel that we were in the ideal place to recharge our batteries. There were deer in the forest that came right up to our picnic table; and the crystal-clear lake was a divine place to commune with the sacred mountain, known to be a portal into the underworld cities of light.

That first night in Mount Shasta, having put the children to bed, Jeremy picked up my *Opening to Channel* book from the bedside table. I had tried to persuade him to read it on several occasions over the previous year, but he had no recollection of ever having seen or heard of it. Although I had just started re-reading it, he was suddenly so passionately drawn to the book that I handed it over. Jeremy had never previously expressed any interest in learning to channel and hadn't been for a single reading, so I was curious what he would make of it.

He got so intensely into the book that he stayed up most of the night reading and then asked me the following morning to give him some space to try some channelling exercises from the cassette tapes. I dutifully went off to the lake with the children to play on inflatable beds in the emerald-green waters. On the way back to our campsite a couple of hours later, I was stopped in my tracks by what I witnessed ahead of me. Jeremy was sitting at the picnic table with his hands clutching the edge, his eyes closed and his head at a distinctly strange angle. I turned around and took the children walking through the woods for another half-hour so as to give him a bit more time. When we finally returned, Jeremy was grinning from ear to ear, almost exploding in his excitement.

My mouth dropped open as he described how, half-an-hour into the exercises, an incredibly strong and clear guide by the name of George had started speaking directly to him. When Jeremy shared the experience with me that evening, I could hardly believe what was happening. My husband had just turned into a channel overnight!

George spoke in a vocabulary and accent that was different from Jeremy's normal speech – just as I had witnessed with other guides who were directly channelled. The answers I received to my questions were of that exact flavour which I had come to recognise and love when I went for a reading. There was an inherent wisdom and "bigger picture" perspective in the information imparted, imbued with an uplifting feeling of unconditional love and respect.

There was no hesitancy on Jeremy's part; the words simply flowed through him. Neither one of us had any doubt whatsoever about the validity of the information he was transmitting. We also knew absolutely that the portal energy of Mount Shasta had facilitated Jeremy's opening to channel. I didn't know at the time that this was also the universe's way of assisting *me* in making that connection.

On our return to London, Jeremy threw himself back into his habitual routine of work, socialising and family life. The magic of his breakthrough in Mount Shasta slowly faded and he practised channelling only when I requested his assistance. I advised him to tape-record the sessions and pay more attention to this gift, but he didn't feel as intensely about it as I did. I recognised that I was superimposing *my* unfulfilled desire to channel on him. His guide, George, told me that I could channel easily if I simply trusted that it was possible. He assured me that my relationship with several guides was already very strong, and just needed to be made conscious.

Witnessing how quick and easy the process had been for Jeremy broke my self-created spell of resistance. I have to confess that I was more than a touch indignant that he had started channelling so effortlessly, when I had tried so diligently, and was so much more passionate about channelling. "If he can do it, I bloody well can too!" said my ego. It was just the kick up the butt that I needed.

My first step was to enrol on an *Opening to Channel* day led by my friends Maggie Pashley and Steven Jewel. In the workshop we practised in pairs, which meant that I was forced to speak out loud in response to my partner's questions. It was stressed that in the beginning stage of practising, you invariably feel like you're making up the answers – which was a natural part of the process. I was indeed uncertain at first if the information was coming from my head or from a higher source, but the feedback from my practice partners was so overwhelmingly positive that I left the workshop greatly encouraged.

My second step was to buy a tape recorder, so as to keep a record of my practice sessions each morning. I grounded myself, expanded my aura, requested that any light beings with guidance for me should step forward, and then asked whatever questions arose in the moment. From the very first day of channelling in this way, a guide called Wanaseh identified himself, coming forward as a beautiful young North American Indian. His words, filled with eloquent metaphors of the natural world, served as loving messages of encouragement on my path. Wanaseh said that we could address our struggles in life "in a light and joyful way, simply by attuning with the higher planes, flowing along them as a bird soars in a current of wind."

I was thrilled to channel Wanaseh; I loved his vibration and imagined that he would always be my personal guide, just as George was for Jeremy. But a few months into my channelling practice I started receiving transmissions from a group of light beings who said that they were a "collective," in that they had a singular purpose or intention. They had much to teach me outside of my personal questions, including how to improve my channelling.

They stressed the importance of asking always for the "highest guidance possible" to flow through me, rather than calling on Wanaseh or any other particular being. That way, they explained, I had the possibility of receiving information from even higher dimensional beings, according to my frequency in any given moment. They advised me not to aspire to be a trance channel, as it was vital that I be present and conscious while I brought the information through. According to them, I was a natural "direct-voice channel" – able to transmit the energy and words of higher beings directly through my body, while staying fully conscious.

Channelling became my first form of personal practice, akin to setting aside time for meditation. I always recorded the sessions, periodically transcribing them onto paper and filing them, which allowed me to look back at the advice given over a long period and gain new perspectives. I wasn't under any pressure to prove the validity of my connection because I channelled only for myself or for Jeremy. It was the most joyful, exciting, life-changing opening I could ever have asked for! Simply by trusting and practising, I was able to receive guidance from a higher realm – without going for readings! My heart-felt wish was fulfilled.

I soon appreciated that travelling to different places facilitated my ability to speak with new guides. When we visited Ireland in the summer of '99, I received communications from a totally new collective that said that they were "of the light of Christos." Part of their message to me was:

> Be not afraid to speak, for it is one of your gifts. Those who will hear your words are starting to gather already. There are many hearts opening which you will assist. Be not afraid that your words are of the ego, for you are one who is a shining pillar of Light!

I had no idea how my channelling might assist others. I knew that I was being guided when I gave advice to my healing clients, but I had no desire at all to give one-on-one readings.

Over Christmas time in France, I received a message from a group of spirit beings called Nirvana, that said I was a part of their collective, and that our mission was to bring the vibration of heaven onto earth. They described themselves as: "blue beings, although in truth the word blue cannot encompass the beauty of our radiance." I was also told by these guides that I would write. They said:

> Your first book will be an expression of the joy you feel in following your path, and will be part of your teaching with those who feel as yet unsure about the meaning of their lives.

And so it is.

CHAPTER 15
Family Healing

The following summer our family holiday destination was Tara Cove in Ireland. The energy there was incredibly high, which stimulated Jeremy and I to practise channelling together one day. We started with an exercise suggested by Sanaya's guide Orin, in which we asked each other questions about our parents.

I knew without a doubt that my parents loved me, and that they had always tried their best for me. Nonetheless, my over-riding experience of childhood was of growing up in an emotional void, which was painful to bear. Throughout my childhood my mother suffered from migraines and periods of depression, which made it difficult for her to be there for her children. She had grown up in a large family where the children were fed and clothed and then left to fend for themselves – it was in her patterning to expect the same of us.

My dad, in the times when he allowed himself to unwind and let go of the worries of the world, was a joy to be with; sociable, funny and engaging. But the stress of his responsibilities; running his own business and coping with my often irrational mother, were always in the background. These factors, combined with his reluctance to show his feelings, meant that he wasn't very approachable when we were young – we girls were fearful of upsetting him, as his temper could snap very suddenly.

I hadn't dwelt much on this in my adulthood; I didn't think there was any need to heal the past. But in Tara Cove when Jeremy's guide described first my mother's and then my father's childhoods, I found tears of compassion for them streaming down my face. He explained that it was simply not possible for either of them to express their love for me fully, and spoke of a way of communicating soul-to-soul with them, despite the fact that they were both still alive. In his words:

Your mother and fathers' souls call out to you from a deep resonant level, to forgive them for time not spent with you. They ask you to accept that this will not be addressed in this lifetime, as they are too set in their ways to be able to change now.

On a spiritual level, they understand how things could have been different, and that if it were not for their years of baggage, they would have made it so different. You must accept them now as they are, with the underlying knowledge that they have been working through very hard lessons.

They ask you to send them light and forgiveness. The more light you send them, the easier the remainder of their life on this earth will be. Send them love; let them know that they have not damaged you in any way, and that you have flown free – a beautiful spirit that has come from their union! Let them know that you will soar and succeed in this lifetime where they have not spiritually gone.

There is little that you could tell them on the physical plane – but much help that you can give them in the inner planes, so that they will achieve the beauty that your soul has very soon. Allow this information to lift you.

This message was so powerful for me. I had never thought about working on a soul-to-soul level with people who were still alive. Receiving such loving messages from the souls of my mother and father was profoundly healing for me. I realised that I had run away from my family in South Africa and hadn't really dealt with the pain of not being nurtured, or being seen as my true self.

Years later, when I knew that my dad didn't have much time left, I travelled to South Africa to say goodbye. He had cancer and had been through a gruelling series of chemotherapy treatments without significant improvement. Although he was in a lot of pain he was still up and about, and totally in denial about his imminent transition. He wasn't willing to talk about it.

I wanted to get closer to him on the trip and to spend as much time with him as possible. I tried to initiate meaningful conversations, but there seemed to be no way in. My mother was being impossible, and the tension in the house was difficult to bear. I felt angry with both of them and wondered why I'd bothered to come. I didn't seem to be able to help, and I certainly wasn't having the quality time with my dad for which I had longed.

One day, sitting on the beach in tears, fragments of the channelling in Tara Cove spontaneously repeated in my mind:

> Your mother and fathers' souls call out to you from a deep resonant level to forgive them. Accept that this will not be addressed in this lifetime, as they are too set in their ways to be able to change now. You must accept them now as they are … they ask you to send them light and forgiveness … the more light you send them the easier the remainder of their life on this earth will be.

A wave of incredible love and compassion swept through me. I remembered the description of their childhoods, and the pain they were both still working through. I realised that I wasn't going to get any closer to my dad. I just needed to accept him as he was, in the moment, and send both him and my mother love and courage on a soul level.

From that moment, my experience of the trip changed. I relaxed into the rhythm of their house with no expectations, simply loving them as much as I could. One afternoon we spontaneously watched some old home movies, laughing at our clothes and hairstyles in the sixties and seventies. We transported ourselves back to the happiest family times we'd shared – on a cruise trip to South America and on a fishing trip in Cape St. Francis on the Eastern Cape coastline.

When I received the news of my dad's death a few months later, I sat down to meditate and connect with him. I sensed instantly that he wasn't in a place to communicate with me directly; my guides said he was still "in transition." But there was a massive sense of relief and joy for both of us.

The joy on his part was in liberation from pain, and relief at the fact that he was *still there*, just without his physical body. On my side, I was over the moon that – once he had achieved the higher perspective which is the inevitable boon of the spirit world – he would be able to see me for *who I really was!* Over the following months, rather than mourning his absence, I felt an increased sense of communion with him. The tears I cried on the day of his death were tears of joy.

CHAPTER 16

Meditation is the Key

A side from my learning to channel, my main spiritual openings
have been through books. One of the early awakeners for me was
The Celestine Prophecy by James Redfield, although my initial reaction
to it was not at all favourable. I had to force myself to continue past
the first three chapters of the adventure fiction because the writing
style was so poor. On the other hand, once I got hooked into the
"prophesies," which were revealed one by one as the story unfolded,
I was captivated!

The book is a spiritual parable designed to awaken the reader to
certain universal truths. On my second read I discerned that the book
was fundamentally about energy; offering lessons in healing, how to
avoid energy drainage and how to replenish our energy directly from
Source.*

Through these teachings I was inspired to become a healer
– as a therapist I wanted to offer my growing clientele something
more than massage and reflexology. I enrolled in a six-month Colour
Healing course which turned out to be a huge disappointment – there
was hardly any hands-on practice and the theory of which colours
had the potential to heal specific parts of the body didn't resonate
with me. My next attempt at attaining my goal was to be initiated into
Reiki Levels I and II. Everyone in the workshop seemed to experience
something remarkable during the initiations and practice sessions, but
I really didn't feel anything. It wasn't that I didn't believe in the power
of Reiki, as I had received some powerful sessions in the past – it just
wasn't my thing.

As a result of these two thwarted attempts at becoming a healer,
I decided to take a more *doctorish* approach, and train in a technically-
orientated discipline. I had heard a lot about Craniosacral Therapy

---

* The book was also teaching about ascension, without explicitly mentioning it. Ascension is the process we are moving
towards, in which we stay on Earth, but become heart-centred beings who exist in energy rather than physical form, like
other higher-dimensional civilisations.

(CST), an offshoot of osteopathy which was becoming well-accepted in mainstream medicine. CST was reported to be remarkable in healing conditions such as migraines, skeletal disorders and depression; and was also being recognised for the benefits that it offered to pregnant women, new mothers, and babies. Having been through my own journey into motherhood, I loved the idea of being able to work with children and pre- and post-natal women.

The training in which I enrolled was far more challenging and time-consuming than I had bargained for – I lived, breathed and dreamt CST for eighteen months. I also cried a lot. It was the first time in my life that I couldn't succeed simply by trying hard. I took copious notes and completed my homework assignments diligently – but it was the practical side that initially flummoxed me. We were instructed to make an energetic cord into the ground, and then centre ourselves in order to "listen" through our hands to the fluid rhythms of the body.

Essentially, we were being told to ground ourselves and move into a state of receptivity – the first part I could just about manage, but my hands wanted to *give* rather than receive. Trying too hard or concentrating too intensely on what you were supposed to be *listening* to was counter-productive. The process only worked when you relaxed and trusted that the client's body could and would communicate with you!

When I finally got the hang of the listening skill, I tapped into an extraordinary phenomenon. I could feel, even from a distance, where something was blocked in the client's body. And then as I held a focus in that place, the body would miraculously respond and initiate the healing, through mobilising the fluids. I knew the theory that therapies such as reflexology stimulate the self-healing ability of the body, but this was my first felt experience of it.

In spite of the complicated anatomy and technical jargon built into the training, CST is in fact healing in the truest sense of the word. The universe had led me towards a path on which I accessed my healing skills only *after* I had given up on my desire to be a healer. This was a lesson in surrender – in letting go of how and when something will be manifested. When we surrender to the higher wisdom of Source, our heart's desires are naturally realised, in the flow.

Practising CST taught me how to "go inside." I discovered that when my clients were *present* in their bodies, it facilitated the healing process – and that the easiest way to keep them in the present moment, was to encourage them to stay with their breath. I would ask a client to slow down her breath, while I breathed in the same rhythm as her. Although I was moving around and doing healing, my soft, rhythmical breath moved *me* into a more receptive and peaceful state of consciousness.

I was increasingly getting feedback from clients about positive life changes they were making because of the guidance they received from me during a session. My guides told me that the time had arrived when I must work with groups of people rather than only one-on-one. This instantly resonated with me – I had been longing to teach some of the skills that had helped me on my own spiritual journey. My first group course was called *Spiritual Connection*, a five-week series of Wednesday evening classes that I taught from home.

I followed the advice from my guides not to plan everything to the last detail. They said that the more spontaneous my teaching was, the more opportunity there would be for *magic* to happen. I did my best to let go of the need to be in control, and as I began teaching "in the flow," the classes unfolded beautifully. The participants who took part loved the content, and I was happy that I'd succeeded in helping them to connect with their spiritual aspect.

When the bookings for my second course were non-existent and I asked for assistance, my guides suggested that I change the title to *Foundation Meditation*. I couldn't quite get my head around that. I protested that I had not been trained in any form of meditation and that I myself wasn't any good at it. They answered, "We offer our guidance – it is yours to accept or reject." It was the sort of reply your parents give you when you're being stubborn and foolish.

I thought back to the final words spoken by Agnes in my very first reading: "Turn negative into positive. Meditation is the key." I had obediently followed through by signing onto a guided meditation course, but I had been bored stiff in the weekly sessions. It seemed impossible to stop my thoughts, and I had come to the conclusion that I just couldn't do it.

In the light of this new guidance to teach meditation, I reflected on the frustrating classes I'd attended all those years ago. Out of the blue a memory arose of my secondary school days, in which I was coaching my fellow school mates for a biology test in the school playground. As this recollection came forward, I heard the words internally, "I am a teacher," and had an epiphany that teaching meditation really was about to be *the key* to my path of service!

It dawned on me that the breath awareness I'd been practising with my CST clients was actually a form of meditation. This was to become a crucial part of my teaching, that *awareness of the breath is a doorway into consciousness.* I got the familiar shiver of anticipation which signified that pieces of the puzzle were fitting into place, and set the wheels in motion for my first *Foundation Meditation* course.

With a little help from my higher dimensional friends, I had just invented a truly awesome new career – as a meditation teacher! I learned to love teaching without preparation, starting a meditation and just riding the wave of inspiration as it arose. My workshops were fully booked, attracting a remarkable variety of students, young and old, from all walks of life. The word spread in the community and I started receiving referrals from the local doctors, who witnessed how many of their patients were being cured of insomnia, panic attacks and depression simply through attending the classes!*

Just as I had become a healer when I'd let go of that desire, so had I manifested my longing to teach after letting go of that dream. This is a basic premise of manifesting your desires – to be crystal clear about that which you wish to manifest – and then to let go of how and when it might happen, leaving space for the universe to work its magic ways.

---

* To experience my Foundation Meditation courses, try these 4 meditations, free to download on my site: 'Blissful Breath,' 'Earth Connection, a Guided Journey,' 'Healing & Balancing Chakra Meditation' & 'Alternate Nostril Breathing.' There are also notes to accompany the practices.

CHAPTER 17

Tripping in the Jungle

In my early years of channelling, my guides spoke repeatedly about Mother Earth and my role in reconnecting people with her. The more I reflected on it, the more I realised that although I appreciated the beauty of nature, I didn't really feel bonded with the earth. I started looking at shamanic books and courses as a potential way to make this connection. Like many other spiritual seekers, I was aware that the shamanic wisdom of the indigenous tribes was re-emerging to assist in the healing of a world gone crazy.

I started off with an *Introduction to Shamanism* weekend workshop hosted by the Sacred Trust in London. Amongst other things, we learned the skill of "journeying" into the other worlds through the trance-like state induced by a regular drum-beat. These worlds, although invisible in our normal state of consciousness, are just as real as our everyday world.

I still found visualisation difficult and I struggled to "travel" to another world as per our instructions. I could imagine myself in another landscape, which was fine as a starting point, but the journey didn't spontaneously take off. I had more success on the second day when we were instructed to ask for a spirit animal guide to lead us on our passage between worlds. That led to an incredible experience with a panther who stared into my eyes so intensely that I found myself physically merging into his body – a shamanic phenomenon called "shape-shifting." As I became one with him, I felt claws sprouting out of my fingertips while he growled the message, "The jungle of the Amazon awaits your presence, shining one!" I was unsure about whether the message was literal, or if it referred to a journey in the shamanic sense, but the awesome panther stayed with me for some weeks in my dreamtime.

My next foray into the shamanic world was a retreat with Brooke Medicine Eagle, a Native American Indian author of *The Last*

Ghost Dance, a book I had enjoyed reading. This was a more intense exploration, a five-day residential workshop on the edge of Dartmoor in the English countryside. I was hugely excited as the workshop approached – looking forward to the teachings that Brooke would pass onto us, the all-night dance, and the walks on the moor in which we would communicate with the great stone beings. As I was to learn repeatedly in my life, when you build up super-high expectations about something, you often have a disappointment coming your way.

I seemed to be the only person who hadn't worked with the teacher before, and I was a bit clueless about what was expected of me. On the very first day I made the blunder of picking up a little wooden bear from a windowsill, causing a horrified silence to descend upon the room. I had apparently touched an animal totem from someone's altar – evidently an unforgivable crime in the shamanic world! The atmosphere was very cliquey, which – as a teacher who went out of her way to be kind and welcoming to beginners – I found grating.

The "ghost dance" preparation involved shuffling around in a circle for hours, until at a certain signal everyone would collapse on the carpet, seemingly unconscious. Having missed the cue, I would belatedly imitate everyone, clumsily falling down, not quite sure what I was meant to be doing down there. In the circle afterwards people would report on the amazing internal journeys they had undertaken, and healings they had received, but I experienced very little of note. The whole workshop started to feel like a joke on me.

The main activity planned for the last day was a sweat lodge – the one thing I had *not* been looking forward to when I initially signed up. The idea of going naked into a cramped outdoor sauna with a group of strangers, and then sitting through a prolonged period of intense heat, sounded intimidating. By the time it came around, however, I felt so let down by the whole workshop that I'd moved into a neutral state of resignation.

My role in the preparation of the lodge was to tramp the grass inside the wood-frame structure into a circular pattern. We would be sitting on the bare earth, and I was to make sure that the surface wasn't stony or uncomfortable. I enjoyed preparing the space, walking barefoot in circles on the ground, creatively laying wild flowers and fragrant leaves in the bare patches. When I eventually took my place in the circle I was tuned into the earth beneath me. For the first time in my life I felt her energy and that of her plants in my body.

In our line-up outside the lodge, I had been wearing a sarong, but once inside we were in total darkness and it felt natural to be naked. As the ceremony unfolded, I found myself increasingly relaxed and immersed in the experience. Glowing red coals were brought in with a long shovel from the fire outside, and we shouted a joyful welcome to each stone as it was placed in the central pit. As our shaman sprinkled dried leaves and herbs onto the coals, sparks flew into the air like a magic spell being cast.

I managed to stay put for all four rounds, lying down occasionally when the heat became too much. Our prayers and songs were so precious that tears streamed down my cheeks. When we re-emerged into the sunlight we all collapsed onto the earth, slowly adjusting to the outside world. Every blade of grass, every cloud that drifted by in the sky, every birdcall, was a sensory revelation. I was reborn into a world of heart-rending beauty.

The sweat lodge made up for all the disappointments that had preceded it. I could not fail to notice that it was once again when I had *given up* and let go of my expectations, that my wish was fulfilled – I had begun my process of connection with Mother Earth.

When I saw an advertisement for a trip to the Amazon the following year, I was reminded of the words of my awesome panther spirit guide who had said that the jungle of the Amazon was "awaiting me." On offer was a two-week group trip to Peru, which incorporated a series of *ayahuasca* ceremonies with Peruvian shamans. Researching the subject, I read accounts of sacred plants that induced amazing visions leading to profound transformation. I looked longingly at photos of shamans brewing sacred potions under towering trees deep in the jungle. The urge to escape suburbia for a potential life-transforming escapade was irresistible.

Jeremy, generous as always, supported my new dream, agreeing to hold the fort on his own for two weeks. In preparation for going wild, I had my hair braided Bo Derek-style, which meant that I wouldn't have to worry about styling it for some weeks. I received inoculation injections for various rare diseases, and set off on my first ayahuasca adventure in early February 2003.

In my romantic daydreams of the Amazon I was sitting in a tropical forest under a glorious star-studded sky, receiving remarkable visions. My first night on ayahuasca was more like a nightmare! I had been warned that I would most likely vomit before the visions started, and I was prepared for that – but what happened instead was that I felt intensely, horribly nauseous, without being able to throw up. No visions, no insights, just extreme nausea coupled with dizziness, for eight straight hours. Some would call that resistance.

We were gathered for the ceremony in a *maloca* – a round wooden room with a roof but no walls, raised up on stilts above the verdant jungle. With the help of my guides I gradually managed to shift my awareness away from feeling sick, and into the beauty of the surrounding nature. I could feel that the plants and animals around us sensed our presence in their territory. It also helped to focus on the shamans' songs, called *icaros* – channelled songs to the plant spirit of ayahuasca, invoking her assistance and cooperation on behalf of those under her spell. The songs were in Spanish, but I understood them from my heart. When one of the shamans stood in front of me and sang a sweet, high pitched melody, I felt an instant release jerk through my body.

As I prepared myself for the second session, two nights later, I tried to let go of any expectations, positive or negative. The medicine took hold half-an-hour after drinking the brew, and I was catapulted into a fast-forward film of my life, starting from childhood and leading to the present moment. I re-lived all the incidents which had caused me pain, one by one, crying my heart out as I suffered through each. Immediately after a specific scene I was shown how – if I simply looked at the situation from a different perspective – no suffering was actually needed. The minute I got the point, *bang* – the next trauma would emerge in the inner film of my life and I would start sobbing again, immersed in the drama. Once again there would be a reprieve in which I was shown a different way of perceiving the event. No matter how difficult the circumstances were, there was always a choice to choose pain or acceptance.

I cried so much that night, I went through two whole rolls of toilet paper. I was apparently releasing repressed pain through snot and tears rather than puking. We had been told to call for assistance when we needed it by firmly calling the name of our facilitator, "Scott!" When I tried to shout for a new roll of toilet tissue, my voice came out in a tiny squeak, inaudible to an ant: "Scott!" I stood up to walk towards him and immediately fell over sideways, completely uncoordinated.

In the early hours of the morning, when the session was over, an assistant walked me back to the *tambo* where I was sleeping. Ever adventurous, I had chosen to live in isolation in the jungle for the two-week period, rather than in a group hut at the base camp. My home was a simple platform with only a grass roof, and a mattress on the floor covered by a mosquito net. On this evening I lived to regret my decision.

After the assistant left me I wearily shined a torch on my bed, only to be greeted with a horrific vision. My mattress was teeming with red ants – thousands of ants covering every inch of my bed in a layer an inch thick. I was too disorientated to make it back to the camp in the dark, and too exhausted to deal with the ants. I collapsed onto the hard wooden floor, wrapped myself in a sheet to try and stave off the mosquitoes, and cried myself to sleep.

On my third ayahuasca journey, the plant spirit graced me with its sense of humour. I had read that ayahuasca could induce psychedelic images of the geometric patterns the local native tribes used in their fabrics. Sure enough, the first thing I saw when the visions started that night were lines of light weaving an intricate design onto a screen in my mind. The patterns had a life of their own, growing into animals, trees and other abstract shapes I didn't recognise.

Once the beautiful tapestry was complete, however, terrifying creatures started to crawl and slither through the holes in the fabric. Snakes, spiders and bugs of every shape and size oozed towards me – and just as I was about to scream with horror, the creepy-crawlies turned into smiley faces! I burst out laughing, giggling until tears once again streamed down my cheeks – only to find the whole scenario repeating itself once more.

When I had been through the terrifying-to-funny routine a few times, I suddenly got the point. I was in charge! The geometric matrix was my mind and I could create a reality which was horrible and frightening, or pleasing and amusing. I started commanding: "Now scary – now funny! Scary – happy!" Every time I succeeded in switching the images I laughed my head off. It was the funniest thing I had ever experienced – and it was coming from my own ability to control my thoughts.

The following day our shamanic leader organised for some women from the local Shipibo tribe to show us how they painted their beautiful fabrics. What I witnessed was incredible! Without any apparent plan or guidelines, they simply started at one corner of the piece of cloth, painting little lines which morphed into intricate geometric designs at an incredible speed. It was literally exactly what I had witnessed the night before when the geometric pattern was painted onto the screen in my mind!

Later, back in safe old London town, I reflected on my ayahuasca journeys during meditation, realising that the plant spirits had been reinforcing a principle I already knew well. I was *always* able to choose my reality, through choosing my perspective – by selecting the lens through which I perceived any situation.

Walking the dogs in Dulwich woods, I spontaneously threw my arms around an ancient oak tree. The exotic jungle that I'd been so desperate to visit couldn't compare with the English countryside that I had grown to love so much. Yogananda's guru taught him that he didn't need to meditate in a Himalayan cave in order to become a yogic master – his small attic room was perfectly sufficient. Likewise, I didn't need to visit the Amazon or consume sacred plants to open my mind – I had my own personal London portal and my own spiritual practice that served the purpose beautifully. The grass is not always greener on the other side.

Exploring on the mighty Amazon

Blessing on the ayahuasca brew

Sunset on the river

CHAPTER 18

Anything Can Be Healed

At the very core of our bodies is a channel of pure light, which is connected by seven energy vortices or chakras along the spine. The word chakra comes from the Sanskrit word for wheel, which relates to the circular flow of energy in each vortex. Chakras generate and regulate the *prana* or life force of which our entire being is made. Each vortex is associated with an aspect of our consciousness; for example, security. When we are focussed on security issues that relate to money, our home or occupation, the root chakra is active. When there is long-term tension around that issue, the chakra will be negatively affected and the parts of the body related to the root, such as the lower back or colon, may suffer also.*

Through simultaneously practising healing and teaching chakra meditation, I had developed a fascination with the relationship between the chakras and the health of the physical body. On one of my visits to the Psychic College I picked up a book called *Anything Can Be Healed*, by Martin Broffman. An American chap in his sixties, Martin taught a method of healing based on what he called the "Mind-Body Mirror System."

I loved the story in Martin's book of how he had healed himself of a terminal spinal tumour. Like Louise Hay and countless other New Age gurus who had been cured of a life-threatening illness, his crisis had led him to the realisation that his disease had originated in his mind – in his thought patterns and beliefs. In his case, he was illuminated whilst on an acid trip, during a Club Med holiday in Martinique!

Sitting at a beach bar relating his tale of woe to the in-house meditation teacher, he received the response: "Cancer comes from

---

* Healing of the chakras can be achieved through simply doing a daily chakra meditation. Try my most popular YouTube offering: Morning Chakra Meditation, a very simple 10 minute practice.

the mind – you need to go to your mind in order to heal it." That statement sparked the epiphany which led to his self-healing. He researched systems to reprogram the mind, discovered the *Silva Method*, and within two months of starting the practice had completely healed himself. One of the visualisations he'd used was of a doctor looking at his scan and exclaiming incredulously, "I don't understand – there's no tumour here!" This was indeed the precise scenario that he ultimately manifested.

What I particularly liked about his story was the approach he adopted during what could have been, on any given day, his last moment on Earth. Rather than detoxing or trying to do all the "right things," he decided that the single criterion he would use when making any choice would be if he was enjoying himself. So he ate and drank whatever he fancied – pepperoni pizza, Twinkies and cola included – and did only what he genuinely felt like. If he was in a conversation with someone that started to bore him, he excused himself. If there was something he thought he might regret not having tried when he died – like taking acid – he tried it. And this philosophy, along with reprogramming his thoughts and beliefs, healed his tumour!

Martin's slogan is: "Do what you want to do, don't do what you don't want to, and trust your trip!" He also insists, over and over again, "Anything can be healed," which is the basis of the philosophy that underlies his Mind-Body Mirror System. In the course of healing himself, he not only mastered how to reprogram his thought patterns, he developed a system of healing through the chakras. I signed up for his four-day program in January 2005, so as to deepen my understanding of the chakras and become a more effective healer. My intention when I enrolled had nothing to do with healing my own body or life – but the universe has its own agenda; its own way of leading us to our highest good.

Seven years previous to this, I had developed a mysterious injury below my left collarbone which intermittently sent my shoulder, neck and upper chest into crippling spasms. Over the years, I had tried every alternative therapy I knew to heal the area, and believed I had just about solved the conundrum. I was on supplements prescribed by a medical intuitive, and I trusted that my problem was on the way out – until I started the *Chakra Healing* workshop.

The very first morning on the bus to the Psychic College, a crippling pain-attack started in the intercostal muscles of my upper chest. It continued right through the introduction that morning in which we were asked to stand up, one by one, and say what we were ready to be healed of. I naturally included the issue at hand – I was suffering so much it was difficult to think of anything else.

The discomfort returned intermittently in the days that followed, making it impossible to ignore the fact that my body was trying to signal to me that something was out of alignment. Despite the fact that I could work out quite easily what other people's symptoms signified, I couldn't get my head around this infuriating pain in my own body.

On a tea-break on the last day, I asked Martin for his thoughts on the matter, indicating the offending area. He said, "That's in-between the throat and heart chakras. What is it that you are not expressing to a loved one about what will make you happy?" He suggested that it might be to do with my husband. I scribbled the question down and thought hard about what I might be hiding from my loved ones, but nothing immediately came to mind. I was generally very open about my feelings with my close family.

I searched my heart about what was going on between Jeremy and me. We had been through a rough patch the previous year when I confronted Jeremy about our sex life – or rather the lack of it. During a long conversation in which I pushed him to the edge in an attempt to understand his withdrawal from me, he confessed: "My worst fear is that I can no longer give you what you need to be happy." He would not be persuaded to explain any further, reassuring me that he still loved me, and still needed my love and support. Believing that he was just going through a difficult period of soul-searching, I stopped pressuring him about sex, and peace reigned once again in the household.

There were two things that helped me to regain my equilibrium in this period. The first was a new manifesting practice I had learnt from Wayne Dyer, where you visualise what you desire while chanting "Aaaaaah" with your exhalation. My guides told me to visualise Jeremy and I sitting opposite each other as our Higher Self aspects. Before chanting, I was to say the affirmation: "I manifest love and peace flowing between Jeremy and me." During the chant, I was to visualise energy in a two-way flow between our heart chakras. Doing this always resulted in my feeling happy and peaceful.

The second was a book I was reading at the time, *Tomorrow's God* by Neale Donald Walsch. It explains that relationships are a vessel into which we ideally place what we wish to receive. If we want support, that's what we give our partner. If we want unconditional love, that's what we put in. This approach struck a chord in me – I could see how beautiful all relationships would be if we learned to operate this way.

When the chakra healing course was over my shoulder pain magically disappeared again, so it was easy to block out what had happened. Although I suspected that the pain had been trying to tell me something, it was easier to forget about it and tell myself that I'd been healed of something unconscious. I was enjoying practising chakra healing with my clients, and therefore decided to do the next level when Martin returned to the UK four months later.

As soon as the second workshop started, the pain crept back into my left shoulder and upper chest. At its worst, a pain attack usually lasted for an hour or so, however this time it persisted more or less continuously throughout the four days. The leading principle of the Mind-Body Mirror System is that every symptom in the body originates from a tension in your consciousness. I believed passionately in this tenet, and had been working with this way of thinking ever since I had read *You Can Heal Your Life*. I knew, therefore, that there was something painful from which I was hiding. By the end of the workshop, there was a feeling of dread in the pit of my stomach.

On the way home, my friend Philly, who had joined me in the course, asked what was upsetting me so much. There was a pause for a few seconds in which I fought an internal battle, before I blurted out: "What if Jeremy isn't in love with me anymore?" She looked shocked and answered, "Don't be silly. Anyone can see that he adores you!" She was repeating what every friend had said to me when I'd been in crisis the year before. "You two could never split up," they'd said. "You're soul mates." I was happy to be reassured.

Jeremy had been away in Scotland for a few days and had just arrived home when I returned that night. We settled down for a glass of wine in the living room after the children had gone to bed. Sitting opposite me on our new Thai floor cushions, Jeremy commented on how exhausted I looked. I was so drained that I had no desire for a deep conversation that night, but in the process of telling him about my shoulder, I spontaneously voiced what I had expressed to Philly at the bus stop; the fear that he might not be in love with me anymore.

A profound silence descended on the room as we looked into each other's eyes. He replied simply, "I am very unhappy with everything in my life right now." I knew instantly that it was true – he was no longer in love with me. Instead of reacting with shock or bursting into tears, I entered into a very still, crystal-clear state of mind. I saw Jeremy from an altered perspective – as if he were a stranger, perhaps a client I was seeing for the first time. Here was a human being racked with guilt and despair. A wave of compassion swept through me for this wonderful man with whom I'd shared the last twenty years of my life.

As I answered him from a place of unconditional love and acceptance, rather than going into a drama of betrayal or despair, he was open-mouthed with surprise. We were both aware that I was responding in a very unusual way. I was reacting to this potentially devastating news from the perspective of my Higher Self, who acts only out of love. My guides and Higher Self had shifted me into a state of consciousness where I could see the bigger picture, and not be triggered into ego reactions. I was also assisted, no doubt, by the many healing sessions I had received during the workshop.

We stayed up all night talking. Jeremy explained as best he could what was going on for him, and it was as clear as day that what he truly needed and wanted was to be set free. I had believed that I knew him so well that it wasn't possible for him to hide anything from me, but it became evident that he had been suppressing his feelings for some time. The prospect of hurting me and the children was so overwhelmingly painful for him that he just couldn't deal with it.

I reassured Jeremy that I would always love and support him, and he returned that promise. We pledged that we would find a way to separate without the children experiencing a "broken family." Within two weeks he had left the house.

I stayed in a state of Higher Self connection for the entire two-week period of our process of separation – and in a milder form, for some months after. It was the most extraordinary thing! When you are in a heightened state of consciousness, it feels as though it will last forever – but in most cases it is temporary. By the time I landed fully back in my personality self, the transition was done and dusted, harmoniously and with as little fuss as possible.

Our break-up was so sudden and unexpected that our friends and families went into total shock. They found it impossible to comprehend my positive attitude and no-fuss approach to our separation. There were members of my close family that I didn't even tell in the first month, because I knew how much disturbance it would cause. I didn't want to be forced to discuss it as if it were a tragedy or a shame, when my perspective on it was entirely positive.

In the end it was *I* who had been hiding the truth from me – subconsciously I had known for a long time that I was living with a man who was no longer in love with me! When you are supressing something which is making you unhappy, you will unfailingly be confronted with it, whether it is through a body symptom or your life circumstances.

Within days of setting Jeremy free, I had the epiphany that I, too, had been set free – free to find love again; free to reinvent my life; free to discover a new me! From the moment of that realisation my shoulder pain disappeared, completely and forever. I truly had manifested love and peace flowing between the two of us, as I had been affirming in my manifesting practice. What a total and unexpected surprise that it had come through our separation – we truly *never* know how the universe will answer our prayers! What can we do but trust and let go, over and over again.

PART 4
Into the Stars

CHAPTER 19

The Pleiadian Connection

As my interest in the channelling process deepened, I inevitably came across books containing transmissions from the Pleiadians. I discovered that from the seventies onwards many channels were spontaneously contacted by these star beings, who hail from the Pleiades constellation. Their civilisation and ours are intimately connected – a fact accepted by all of Earth's indigenous people, who considered this star race their brothers and sisters in the skies. Tribes scattered across the globe, long before global communication was possible, had similar names for the constellation – the *Seven Sisters*, or in the case of the Maoris, the *Mother with Six Daughters*.

It wasn't the Pleiadians' star origins which attracted me to these books, however – I was indifferent to extraterrestrial phenomena – my desire was simply to receive enlightening information from the wisest guides to whom I had access. What drew me in was the completely different and fascinating perspective the P's provide on the past, present and future of life on planet Earth.

The first book that found its way into my hands was *The Pleiadian Agenda* by Barbara Hand-Clow, which simultaneously fascinated and freaked me out. I could *feel* the power and truth that radiated from the words of Satya, the primary Pleiadian individual who speaks through the author. Some of the material in the book, however – such as the tales of lizard beings who disconnected our DNA in order to control us – left me feeling uneasy and confused. When I asked for guidance on whether I should continue reading the book, I was told:

> This book is of an unsuitable depth for your current understanding – it will present itself to you in a different way, at a time when it is more appropriate. The Pleiadians will eventually lift you higher, higher than the planes of Ashkanaza, which will lead you to find a deeper understanding of your own relevance in the world.

Every hair on my body stood on end at those words. I couldn't imagine what they meant, but the message filled me with excitement.*

As I persisted in my channelling practice, I occasionally had a surreal new experience. In the middle of a session, a guide would come forward and *sing* a message through my voice, in a sort of rhyming poem. In my first singing communication I was told something that I was in no way ready to hear – that I had been taken onto an alien spaceship when I was just four years old!

I wasn't prepared to contemplate the reality of aliens or spaceships in my life, and quickly blocked the incident from my mind. I had never questioned where Sanaya's guide Orin hailed from; or, if Nirvana – the group of blue beings I had channelled in Ireland – was from the stars. I put them all in the category of light beings, or guides from a higher dimension.

The next Pleiadian book I discovered was *Bringers of the New Dawn,* the first in a wonderful trilogy channelled by Barbara Marciniak. Through these three books I came to love and respect the Pleiadians enormously; they were fun, funny, way-out, and paradoxically also very down to Earth. This opening of my heart to the P's precipitated a wonderful encounter with them in the Balham clinic where I practised.

While grounding myself in preparation for a craniosacral client, I was suddenly surrounded and transfixed by an intense blue-white light, receiving what my guides later called a "Pleiadian activation." During the transmission that followed I was told, amongst other things, that I would eventually move into a Pleiadian-inspired type of healing. But the actual *feeling* of their energy was more significant for me than the information I was given. I was literally showered with pure love, and transported into a state of complete bliss.

I was ecstatic about this direct contact with the P's, floating around on cloud nine for the rest of the day. But there was no one in my life with whom I could share this awesome initiation. Jeremy was

---

* Satya's model of the dimensions within our Milky Way Galaxy details how the physical, third dimension in which we live (3-D), relates to the dimensions of the inner earth (1 to 2-D), and the non-physical dimensions above us (4 to 9-D). The Pleiadians themselves live in the fifth and lower sixth dimensions – a more advanced, heart-centred world, invisible to us, but nonetheless as real as our own. This model was to prove invaluable to my experiences and teachings in later years.

always supportive, but anything to do with extraterrestrials was too "out there" for my friends to accept – never mind my being activated by a group of aliens! I was consoled and encouraged, however, by a message I received soon after the activation.

> In the New Age which comes, you will be free to speak about us – your intuition will allow you to know when it is appropriate. We Pleiadians are with you all the time. Ours is the soft energy you describe as the heart chakra energy. We have joined you to co-create a reality in which love becomes the primary focus on Earth. Use your power and energy to spread this vibration in any way which it is possible to do.

I wanted nothing more than to help co-create a more peaceful and loving reality on the planet, and I made a resolution to overcome any blockages that might be holding me back from being of service in this way.

After reading about rebirthing in a book by Bob Frissell, I was inspired to go for a series of sessions. Rebirthing is a therapy invented by Leonard Orr which involves being guided into a continuous, circular breathing pattern, inducing a trance-like state. As memories and feelings arise you simply breathe through them, releasing old patterns and pain that have been stuck in both your emotional and physical body.

In one of the sessions – the one to which I refer in Chapter Two of this story – I spontaneously travelled backwards in time to the age of four, to the very incident about which I'd been told in the afore-mentioned singing transmission. I found myself standing in my childhood garden looking up at a beam of light which emanated from a light ship hovering above the house. After accepting a telepathic invitation to visit the craft, I had the wonderful sensation of being sucked into a tunnel of energy in which my body no longer felt physical. The next minute I was in the vessel, communicating through thought-transference with a group of luminous and loving light beings – humanoid beings literally made out of a glowing energy. After a wondrous interlude during which we exchanged information, love and laughter, there was a "skip forward," and I was suddenly back on the large expanse of green lawn, watching the space craft dematerialise. The child-me started to cry, confused and disorientated.

When the flashback receded, I felt myself in my adult body again, on the mattress, in my therapist's room. This was something I couldn't process with my rebirther after the session – she wanted to work through emotional issues, while I wanted to talk to my star friends! I raced home on my bicycle, locked myself in my healing room and announced to my guides that I was finally ready to know the truth about what had happened. Their response referred back to the original poem-song I had channelled.

> You were indeed taken 'way up high, into the sky'
> – into another dimension, where the beings were
> unfamiliar in Earth terms. These beings of light
> *did* experiment with your consciousness, but with
> no intent to harm. There was an aspect of you
> which was left 'out in the cold,' so to speak, after
> this experience, and this does partly explain your
> alienation from your family as a child. More than
> this it is not necessary or desirable to know, and it
> is not something on which we wish you to dwell.
> Simply know that all is well in your world.

This message, combined with the information I received a few months later, filled in the blanks. In the third channelling, the Pleiadians told me for the first time that the ship on which I had been received was one of theirs. The voice I channelled was sweet and clear, their trademark signature in their future communications. They closed with the words:

> We are here, have no fear, green and blue are with
> you. We say farewell now from our ship, where you
> have been before. You were a willing participant in
> an experiment of a meeting of energies between

extraterrestrials and earthlings. It was necessary to work with children, whose imagination and 'sight' were not yet impaired. And although we do apologise for leaving you 'homeless' after this experience, we say 'praise be' that this allowed you to disentangle yourself from family politics, and to be where you are meant to be today. Hold your head up high – conduct yourself with grace and dignity, as it behooves you, a true goddess and leader, a beacon of the light.

They explained that the experiment in which I had been involved had included a scanning of the mental and emotional fields of all willing human participants. Their purpose had been to determine what was restricting Earth people's spiritual evolution, at the exact moment in history when it was crucial for our evolution to accelerate.

In my case, they had immediately spotted that I was trapped in a fear-inducing karmic conflict with one of my parents, which was likely to continue over-riding my soul purpose for this incarnation. They had offered to help resolve the situation by removing certain incidents from my memory bank, thereby cutting the effect of the karmic cord. I willingly gave my consent, trusting them implicitly.

From the broader perspective that my guides now offered, I could see that the feeling of alienation which had resulted from this incident was in many ways a blessing. And more important still, through the flashback I had joyfully reconnected with my Pleiadian star family, who had been waiting patiently for me to remember my commitment to assist them in their mission to awaken the people of Terra.

CHAPTER 20

Freedom

After separating from Jeremy, I experienced a surge of excitement and adventurousness, revelling in my newfound single status. Jeremy was happy to move back into the house whenever I wanted to go away – he missed the home into which he had put so much love, and seized any opportunity to spend more time with the children. To my delight, I discovered that rather than having less freedom as a single mum, I had more!

My first adventure in the spring of 2005 was a shamanic community retreat in the Welsh countryside. In the stunning mountains of Mid Wales, sixteen of us slept in communal yurts, practising the rituals of our forefathers and sharing stories around the fire. It was wonderful living off-grid with no electricity or running water, the group functioning as a community in which our different skills were shared.

Washing naked in the icy mountain streams and walking through the bursting spring countryside were sensory delights that recharged and awakened my body. Newly single and with raging hormones, I found myself one glorious morning up in the mountains entwined with a fellow tribesman. We made passionate love beside a waterfall on a mossy bank amidst the hollyhocks – an experience of absolute nirvana.

The man in question turned out to be totally unsuitable as a boyfriend, but the interlude made me yearn for someone with whom to share my love once more. In typical new-divorcee style I dove headlong into a series of relationships, none of which really fed my soul, and all of which distracted me from my spiritual goals.

My restless spirit yearned for more adventure, but I recognised the need to refocus spiritually, and planned my next journey with that in mind. I decided to visit India for a month, the longest time I had ever been away from the children. I'd always wanted to go to the

East, and chose it at this juncture in order to bring my focus back to my path, and away from boyfriends. My guides said that there was an important teacher I would connect with there, and all that was needed to manifest him on my journey was my clear intention.

Nothing can prepare one for India. Looking at pictures and hearing people's stories can't convey the feeling that one experiences of having stepped off the "normal" world. My first revelation came within minutes of landing on the streets of Delhi.

A few years previous to the trip, I'd started using the Sanskrit greeting *Namaste,* which means "I bow to the Divine in you." I had instigated a ritual at the end of my meditation classes where the group Namaste'd each other, one at a time. One evening just before leaving for India, I spontaneously voiced in my class how wonderful it would be to live in a reality where people greeted each other in this loving, respectful way every day.

Please bear in mind that I had absolutely no idea that Namaste actually *was* the greeting used all over India. When I walked through Delhi that first morning and was greeted with a full Namaste by nearly every person I passed, including the bowed head and prayer mudra, my jaw dropped in amazement! I felt as though I had magically manifested exactly what I'd wished for – a world where everyone openly acknowledged each other as divine beings of light!

In every other way, however, my arrival in Delhi was a nightmare. Following the recommendation of the *Lonely Planet India* travel guide, I tried to catch a taxi to a hostel that was described as a favourite hangout for backpackers. Instead, my taxi driver took me to an agency, saying that it was necessary to pre-book the hostel. I had fallen for one of the typical scams where, after making a fake call, the agent says there's no room at the inn, subsequently trying to get you to book a hotel or a guided trip on which he's getting a commission.

By the time I finally extricated myself from the scoundrels and found my way to the hostel I was frazzled and exhausted – not to mention freezing! The last thing I'd been expecting in India was to feel cold, but Delhi that January was sub-zero at night, and I had come totally unprepared. My room in the run-down hostel was a cold cement jail cell with large holes in the wall and no windows. I collapsed onto my rock-hard mattress fully dressed including my shoes, tossing and turning all night in an effort to keep warm. I had planned to stay for two nights, but by the following morning, had made up my mind that I was getting out of Delhi as soon as possible.

Where to go, was the question. I had been instructed by my guides not to make any plans past my arrival, and to use the following mantra as my affirmation for the whole trip: "I am led to the perfect places, people, and experiences for my highest good." Suspecting that in this instance it would be a person who guided me to my next port of call, I sat down at the communal outdoor breakfast table waiting for my messenger. Within a few minutes I was joined by an enigmatic Englishman in his sixties with a dapper silver moustache, stiff white hat and walking cane, who ordered some traditional English tea. He introduced himself formally, and proceeded to tell me a bit about his recent travels in the Himalayas. Just as I was about to ask for a suggestion of where I might begin my travels, he placed his newspaper firmly in front of his face and went out of view.

Reluctant to interrupt him, I waited all the way through breakfast for him to talk again, but he appeared to be fully immersed in his paper. Somewhat disheartened, I finally stood up and began walking away. When I was half way back to my room he suddenly looked up and shouted after me, "I think you should go to Pushkar young lady, you'll like it there" – and up went the paper again! With a huge grin on my face I wrote down the name of the town, slung my backpack on and went straight to the train station. Within an hour I was heading for Pushkar in Rajasthan, 244 miles south of Delhi.

The yurt camp in rural Wales

My yurt beside the stream

Hollyhocks and lush mountains

My first day in India – magical Namaste's

Around a fire – chilly Delhi January

CHAPTER 21

In Search of Babaji

On the train journey to Pushkar, surrounded by Indian families, I looked up my new destination in a guidebook. I was thrilled to discover that this town, nestled around the banks of a sacred lake, was considered one of the five holiest pilgrimage sites in the whole of India. According to Hindu scripture, the lake was created when Lord Brahma slew the demon Vajranabha with his weapon: the lotus-flower. In this process lotus petals fell to the ground, creating three holy lakes, Pushkar Lake being the middle one of the trinity.*

It is said that when Brahma descended to Earth, he decided to perform a fire ceremony or *yagna* at Pushkar Lake. His wife Savitri couldn't join him at the appointed hour for the ritual, and so he married a local woman from the Gayatri race, completing the yagna with his new consort sitting beside him. When Savitri finally arrived and found Gayatri sitting in *her* rightful place, she cursed Brahma, decreeing that he would be worshipped only in Pushkar. Thus it is that the temple in town dedicated to Brahma is the only one of its kind in the world.

When I arrived in Pushkar in the late evening, I was instantly enchanted. I found a room in the Lotus Hotel on the far bank of the lake with a veranda overlooking the water, and settled in to stay. I felt sure that this was the place where I would find the teacher of whom my guides had spoken. I had to chuckle when I realised that I had been guided to a town where there was no opportunity for me to party and lose my way. The sacred town of Pushkar was completely free of alcohol, meat and even eggs; the dress code was strictly modest, and devotion to the many faces of God was embedded into all aspects of life.

---

* In Hinduism the formless supreme God is made of a triad of deities: Brahma the creator, Vishnu the preserver, and Shiva the destroyer or transformer.

Everyone in town honoured the custom of removing their shoes respectfully on the steps of the *ghats,* the bathing places on the lake's edge. The locals and pilgrims took the waters at sunrise and sunset, men and women bathing separately. The men stripped down to loincloths or shorts, while the women washed discreetly without removing their clothes – magically moving layers of their saris in practised rhythms in order to maintain their modesty.

I learnt from the locals that bathing in the waters of certain ghats had the potential to gift one with special gifts: the Naga Kund Ghat bringing fertility, the Roop Tirth gifting beauty and charm, and the Mrikand Muni Kund endowing wisdom. Reluctant to presume I could bathe with the locals, I used a quiet place on the banks of the lake in the early dawn. I paid my respects to the water spirits, to the ancestors and to Brahma himself in my daily ritual.

My favourite place on the outskirts of town was Ratangiri Hill, home to the Savitri Temple. The steep walk up was a challenge at first, but the glorious view overlooking the town and lake made it worth the sweat. Although the temple itself was delightful, my favourite place to hang out was on the hillside behind it where mountain birds glided past on the wind currents. Aside from me, only the local women and children ventured here, collecting wood for their fires and doing their daily chores.

A short while into my month in Pushkar I started a yoga class led by a humble teacher from Ajmer, named Shyam Sunder. His classes were held outside in a dirt yard, surrounded by trees that were constantly filled with parakeets. I wasn't particularly impressed with his teaching of the yoga postures, but I persisted because of the breathing and meditation practises that comprised the last half-hour of the class. He was teaching interesting forms of chakra meditation, combining them with breathing techniques completely unfamiliar to me. He was also leading guided visualisations which seemed to be a form of astral travelling; pulling your consciousness into a point of light and then travelling into the heavens. Shyam insisted on calling me "madam" and would say in an impassioned manner, "And now madam, be seeing yourself sitting in a golden chariot next to the great

Krishna himself!" – which would make it hard not to giggle. Despite his slightly eccentric English and style, I really did feel the potency of the journeys through which he guided me.

When Shyam realised that I was more interested in the meditation and pranayama than the physical asanas, he instructed me to come an hour earlier than the regular morning class so that he could teach me more effectively one-to-one. He also insisted that I do certain practises before coming. It took a lot of willpower to set my alarm for 5 a.m. every single morning, being that I was on holiday. But if I complained at all, Shyam laughed, telling me that for countless years, he had been doing his spiritual practises from 4 till 6 a.m. before going to work. He reminded me often that the result of his discipline was that he was in a permanent state of joy. He also foretold that I would one day teach some of the techniques that I was learning from him to my own students.

In my last week in India I was captivated by a book I was given, entitled *Autobiography of a Yogi*. There are certain books that are better read whilst in the country where the story is set, and this is most definitely one of them. I wondered as I read it whether the author, Paramahansa Yogananda, was actually the teacher that my guides had predicted for me. As it transpired, it was the synchronistic fusion of his teachings and Shyam's that opened the doorway to my true teacher; the beloved Mahavatar, Babaji.*

Yogananda explains that Babaji is a manifestation of God who has chosen to stay on Earth to help us. He is acknowledged as an immortal master who has shown himself in many different physical forms over the past few thousand years. Through one of his embodiments, a lineage of teachers emerged who were initiated by him into some of the very techniques which Shyam had passed on to me. Reading the book brought a whole new level of understanding about the gifts I had received while in Pushkar. Yogananda taught me that these *kriya* techniques, in a more advanced form, were the very ones used by Jesus, Elijah and other prophets to materialise and dematerialise their bodies at will.

---

* Watch the wonderful film *AWAKE: Life of Yogananda* to learn more about Yogananda and Babaji.

Returning to London in the dismal winter grey of February was a difficult adjustment. As I walked my dogs in the park I was shocked at the lack of colour and sound after the vibrant wall paintings, saris, spices, flowers, markets, cows and motorbikes on the streets of India. It looked to all intents and purposes as if the colour had been sucked out of the world and I had landed in a black and white movie.

During a self-led rebirthing session in my healing room one morning, I burst into tears as a deep feeling of loneliness washed over me. My thoughts turned to Babaji, remembering that he is said to appear unfailingly when one calls for his assistance with a pure and open heart. Spontaneously I cried out, "Babaji, do you really come when someone calls?" A crash of electricity audibly hit the room.

The shift of energy was so sudden and strong that I opened my eyes in surprise. As I looked up at the pink and gold silk ceiling tapestry, Babaji in his full body descended into the room through the fabric. He hovered above me for a few precious minutes, lovingly smiling into my eyes. Into the profound silence he sang:

You just call out my name
And you know wherever I am
I'll come running, to see you again
Winter, spring, summer or fall
All you have to do is call
And I'll be there
You've got a friend

I have not experienced anything else as beautiful as this materialisation of Babaji, before or since – it was a gift beyond measure. He was literally answering my question, and – along with the love and compassion he showered upon me – his response revealed an undeniable sense of humour. When I initiate students into the kriya cobra breath I always tell them about my meeting in the flesh with the immortal master. It rates right up there with my most powerful and surreal encounters: Babaji singing a Carole King song to me – not in India, but in the suburbs of South East London!

Babaji in the embodiment of which
Yogananda speaks

In his Haidakhan embodiment, as he
showed himself to me

Men taking the waters at a ghat

Women in the market

Pushkar from Ratangiri Hill

The sacred lake of Pushkar

Meditation on the roof of the Lotus Hotel

My photos in India were filled with orbs

With the hippy gang in Pushkar

One of the bathing ghats

CHAPTER 22

Pleiadian Mission a-Go-Go

Not long after my trip to India my guides announced, "This is the time that has been spoken of, in which you reconnect with the Pleiadian vibration." Having received so much positive assistance through the books I had read, I was now keen to know if I could channel the Pleiadians directly. My guides said that in order to achieve that, I would have to purify myself through diet and energy practices. As I automatically started thinking about living the life of a nun, they added, "This does not mean, however, that you stop having fun!" Rather than a consolation clause, this was an important aspect of their guidance – that I must have fun in the process of purifying myself.

They suggested that the most important substances to eliminate from my diet were meat (which they called "dead flesh") and alcohol. They said that meat was the primary food that was causing my vibration to be too dense, and that alcohol was the substance causing the swings in my mood and energy. I asked about including fish in this cleanse, and my guides said simply, "Fish is flesh." They stressed that rather than having the attitude that I was depriving myself, I should focus on choosing delicious foods and drinks that held the maximum light quotient, to "en-lighten" my body and frequency.

Excited by the assurance that my purification would lead to a more direct Pleiadian contact, I made a formal vow to myself to do whatever necessary to accomplish this. As my guides heard this telepathically, they replied, "We shall talk to you when you have fasted in this form for ninety days." This promise was fulfilled, and my experience of the Pleiadians on the ninetieth day was as overwhelming as it had been three years before in my "activation." The transmission began in the form of a song, in the sweetest of voices, gradually shifting to ordinary speech.

Waves of energy and light we bring to you; waves of peace and harmony too. Waves of love to open up your heart – to see the gifts before you, to see the gifts before you, to see the gifts before you.

We come on waves of light to your planet, in this space and time which is the twenty-first century on the earth plane. We have a meeting with you – from far away, from long before – which is destined now to be. We meet with you and all of the children of Earth who reside now in this dubious plane. We call it dubious because you are filled with doubts as the human race, about your purpose; your function. We call it dubious because the plane is shifting as we approach 2012. Even now, this year of 2006 is one in which huge shifts occur, if one can but be aware.

We speak to you as a group of light beings who work on Earth now. You are one of our group, though you may not be aware. We ask you to work with groups, as you begin to do now.

Over the following months I asked for the Pleiadians to communicate with me, and they did – but not so much with new information. What I received several times felt like an energy shower of their loving vibration, usually with a vision of coloured lights. As much as I cherished these experiences, I was frustrated at not being able to channel information from the Pleiadians in the way I did from other guides. A sense of anticipation was growing in me, however, and I knew that when the time was right I would have the full connection with them that I had come to unequivocally desire.

Early 2007 found me packing my bags once more, this time for South Africa, to visit my mother who was seriously ill. I decided to spend time with my eldest sister Gail in Johannesburg first, and then fly to Knysna where both my mother and sister Darrell had settled. I hadn't been to South Africa since my father's passing, and felt some guilt about the distance I'd put between myself and my remaining family. When my guides said that the time spent in my country of birth would precipitate a significant healing of the past, I assumed that this had to do with my family. They told me that I would need to stay centred in order to accomplish "my given mission."

On my first night in Johannesburg, struggling to get to sleep, I decided to sit outside in Gail's garden under the full moon to channel with my trusty tape recorder. My guides came through immediately, with the words:

> We ask you to connect with the land every day without fail, understanding that this land is your heritage, your birthright. This connection with Africa which you have severed will come into play in time, when the wounds of the past are healed, and you are with another man.

In bed a short while later I wondered about the man that had been mentioned, tuning into the juiciest bit of the message and ignoring the rest. I was in holiday mode, and fell asleep fantasising about a romance with a lovely blonde, long-haired hippy in Knysna, blissfully unaware of my guides' agenda for me.

It was five days before I channelled again, being busy with family reunions and travelling to Knysna. I was experiencing the usual disconnect from my spiritual path that beset me on trips to South Africa. I was totally taken aback when my guides came through with an unprecedented tone of urgency, sounding much like the commanders of a battalion issuing orders to their troops before battle!

> We align you now – with not only the universal energy flow, through your kundalini line – but also with your purpose; and your purpose in South Africa in particular. You imagine that you are here to be forgiven, and to forgive your family members. This may be part of what happens on this trip, but more important than this – there is an energy flow

which we ask you to tap into in this part of Earth,
and to do this as frequently as possible.

I was astounded when they proceeded to give me a numbered list of very specific instructions:

1. To phone the meditation teacher whose leaflet I had randomly picked up the day before.
2. To visit the highest geographic location in the area, "known to be a spiritual vortex."
3. To go to a place called Coney Glen, which they described as "a place of great power and mystery."
4. To meditate with the moon and stars every night.
5. To draw light into the space in which I was living every day.
6. To visit my mother in the morning or evening, leaving time to do the spiritual work which I had "neglected so far."

I was clueless as to what was meant by "tapping into the energy flow," but the specific instructions were hard to ignore. I had only nine days left in Knysna, and suspected that I wouldn't be back for a few years. The fact that I had a very particular purpose while I was in the country spurred me into action. This was the third time I'd been told that the primary purpose of this trip was an acceleration of my path. I needed to stay focussed, do my daily practices and keep in touch with my guides.

Although I suspected that the first three instructions had been given in that order for a reason, I was reluctant to act on the first directive, to phone the meditation teacher. I wasn't keen to join a class, and didn't know what we would talk about. As for the second instruction, I asked myself how I was expected to find this very particular location. I had no metaphysical friends in Knysna and I somehow doubted that the tourist office would be able to help. On top of that, the day was already hot, which made the idea of mountain climbing unappealing. I decided instead to start my mission that day by going to Coney Glen, which was third on the list – at least I knew where that was.

My guides had other ideas.

CHAPTER 23

Homeland Activation

I was in my hire-car ready to set off when I realised that I'd left my sunglasses behind. Back in the house in the process of looking for them, I *twice* knocked the meditation class leaflet off the side table, the second time actually slipping on it when I stood up to leave. "Okay okay I get the message," I laughed, sitting down to phone the teacher, who was called Rebecca. From that point on, synchronicities started flowing in a mind-blowing way.

When I asked what type of meditation she was teaching, Rebecca replied that the class that week was unusual in that it was going to take place outdoors in a very special location. When I asked where they were going, she explained they would be climbing up to "the highest point in the surrounding area" – a place called Spitzkop, considered to be a powerful *spiritual vortex!* Step number one accomplished; step number two a-go-go!

When I heard about Spitzkop, a shiver shot straight down my spine and my lethargy evaporated. I was on a mission, assisted every step of the way, and I committed to following the guidance I was given to the tee. Now that I knew where I needed to go, I drove straight to the tourist office to get a map and headed off on my assignment. Within an hour, I was bumping down a pitted dirt road through a huge forest reserve.

Half-way there, I spotted a sign pointing off to the left that read: "King Edward VII Big Tree." Being particularly fond of big trees I spontaneously veered off the track, and five minutes later found myself staring up into the distant crown of a stunning 800-year-old yellowwood tree. There was a low barrier around the tree to protect it, which I couldn't resist stepping over. I heard Jeremy's voice in my head, "There she goes, breaking the rules as usual," which made me laugh.

I Namaste'd to the great tree, requesting permission to enter into its huge aura, and then tuned into my guides to ask if I should meditate here or go straight onto Spitzkop. To my surprise they said, "You are now in one of the power spots which you were seeking in this area, and with this tree you align yourself energetically with the flow which leads you forward on your path." I gathered that channelling would be more appropriate than meditation, but when I sat down to channel, I was told to stand up again. My instructions were: "In this place, channel energy directly through yourself and into Earth, and an opening with the Pleiadians will come. Do this now."

I stood up with my back to the tree, not quite touching, and closed my eyes. As I uttered an invocation to ground myself, a channel of bright white light, like a lightning bolt, shot straight up from the body of the tree into the sky. Immediately following this I felt a similar light flow through me – the tree had opened a portal in which I was totally encompassed!

As instructed, I allowed the energy to flow through my body into the earth. I was transfixed, standing very straight with my arms out to the side, my body rocking back and forth in a flowing light that permeated my every cell. When there was a sense of completion I sat down again, totally blown away by the experience. Remembering the forthcoming opening that I'd been promised, I prepared myself to channel once more.

The Pleiadians spoke through me instantaneously – for the first time with a fluid transmission of information, like my usual guides:

> You make a connection with the Pleiadians and with
> Earth in this place. You understand now that calling
> light to yourself is more than just wishful thinking.
> It is a means in the New Age of awakening yourself
> – and awakening is what you do now!

I had adopted the practice of "calling light to myself" after reading the Marciniak books, and had taught it regularly in my meditation classes. These guides were explaining that there were energy exercises that I had previously understood only on a theoretical level, without actually experiencing their purpose.

In a state of intense anticipation, I asked the Pleiadians if they could tell me what their purpose was with me, or what my purpose was with them. They replied jokingly:

> You hit the nail on the head now, sweet Earthling,
> as you realise with your wording that our purpose is
> as one. Our purpose, yours and ours, is as one – it is
> the purpose of awakening the human race.

I found my head nodding involuntarily, as it often did when I channelled, and they explained that this was a by-product of their energy flowing through me. They encouraged me to bring it through all of my chakras, and not just my throat.

When I drew their energy right down through my root chakra I felt a distinct shift; a much stronger flow through my body. The P's responded: "This is better, this is better. This is fun, is it not?" And it was! I suddenly saw the Pleiadian collective as a swirling combination of sparkling green and turquoise lights. I was *in* the ocean-like energy, and it encompassed me completely. The colours and the experience were so beautiful that I found tears pouring down my cheeks. They continued:

> We flow through you now, and do this formally as
> an awakening, in order that you channel for others
> in a group. We ask you to be brave, in advertising:
> *Channelling the Pleiadians & Awakening the Light Body.*

I was being asked to teach two new Pleiadian courses when I returned to England, and the wording I was to use in advertising them followed, flowing like poetry, with a clear sense of when each new line was introduced:

> Come those who have awakened to their spirit path;
> those who feel a connection with other life forms in the universe;
> those who wish love and light to flow through them as channels
> for the awakening of mankind on this sweet Earth we inhabit.

Accompanying this second Pleiadian activation, I was being shown how my alliance with the star people would assist in my future role as an awakener for my Earth tribe! Feeling as high as a kite, I hugged the tree, thanking him for his help with my activation.

As I flung my arms around a small section of the huge trunk I distinctly heard the tree ask for my assistance. He said that a "cancer being" was feeding off his roots, and asked if I would be so kind as to remove it. Stunned at having heard such a specific message from a tree, I stepped backwards and looked down at the exposed roots, immediately spotting an ugly white fungus. Nervously looking around to check that no one was present, I tried unsuccessfully to prise it off – it was embedded as if it had been super-glued on. Fishing in my backpack, I laughed out loud for the third time that day at the synchronous events supporting my journey. Darrell had just that morning given me my dad's treasured old pen knife to take back to London as a keepsake. I thanked my dad as I used it for the first time, asking for guidance as I performed what felt like emergency surgery.

I bowed to the tree on completion, sensing his gratitude, before racing back to the car. I needed to drive to Spitzkop, climb the hill, do whatever I was meant to do and still get back before dark. To my relief I was able to drive most of the way up the hill, soon finding myself on a grassy mound taking in the panoramic views in all directions. I was told, "This place is a transducing point, where energies can be 'stepped down' to heal Earth. Once again, raise your arms, and allow the energies to flow through you and into Earth."

My body was rocked again, this time in a back and forth dolphin-like motion, getting faster and stronger. Alone on the hilltop, totally at one with the earth on which I stood, I let out a deep *Aaaaaah* sound, allowing my body to be moved by the stupendous energy flowing through me. When I sat down and started to channel, I was shocked by the deep booming voice that came out of my mouth.

> This is the beginning of a new connection for you; a new guide. My name is Amatron. This is of Egyptian origin, and my purpose with you, as with the Pleiadians, is to help raise your vibration to a point where you are doing your life's work in

transmuting the energy of this Earth plane. Is it
not powerful to feel yourself being moved by the
energy of all-that-is-above and all-that-is-below? Is
this not your true purpose – to bring the energy of
Heaven onto Earth?

I am Amatron. My incarnation on this Earth
plane was as a powerful healer in Atlantean times.
I was present too in the Egyptian incarnation in
which you accessed the Amatron energy – in
which you used this energy for the healing of the
people. But you were not yet aware at that time of
your greater purpose, which is not with individual
healing, but with global energy shifting, and the
bringing through of this vibration.

I was mesmerized by this new guide and would have loved to
have stayed up on the hill longer; however, by this time the sun was
nearing the horizon and I needed to start on my way back. My head
was reeling as I made my way home, bumping along the darkening
dusty road through the pine forests. The two sets of guides I'd
channelled were fascinating, both extremely strong and clear, yet
so different. The Pleiadian guides had a gentle, feminine quality
when they spoke through me, whereas Amatron sounded distinctly
masculine and authoritative. The *feeling* from both of them, however,
was very loving.

As is often the case when I channel, I couldn't absorb everything
I'd been told immediately. I was more focussed on the astonishing
physical experiences I'd had, both at the Big Tree and at Spitzkop.
The energy streaming through me simultaneously from above and
below had nearly knocked me off my feet! It was the first time in
my life that I had really felt Earth's energies in my body, and I was
profoundly moved.

Exploring Coney Glen the following day as instructed, I came
across a cave that had been used by local witch doctors. There

were piles of bones scattered in groups on the sand floor, and the atmosphere was intimidating. For the first time, I channelled the consciousness of a shaman. He had lived in the cave "many moons before," and was accessible to me only because I was able to connect with his energy field on a fourth dimensional level. This was a skill that was to come to the fore often in my later work, and which required a high level of discernment on my part. It is essential to be able to determine whether or not it is appropriate to channel ancestor spirits who present themselves – they are not always of the light. In this case, the shaman was not evil, but he had nothing to teach me and I was keen to get out of there.

Emerging into the fresh sea air, I stood on the windy cliff-slope above the rocks and asked for guidance about my next step, unsure why I had been asked to visit Coney Glen. The channelling was suddenly interrupted as my upper body was physically jerked backwards, chest to the sky. I felt the energy of a strong, stately woman overtake me and my voice assumed the commanding tone of a queen, crying out, "Oh Akhenon! Oh King of Kings! My heart weeps with the death and demise of your spirit." Immersed in the drama of the moment, tears coursed down my face and I momentarily felt her heartache as an actual physical pain in my chest.

As my body slowly straightened up and I returned to the present, Amatron explained that I had been assisted in revisiting a past life; a lifetime in Egypt in which I had been a priestess. In the flashback I was mourning the death of a pharaoh whose friendship had afforded me power. The synchronicity sparking this past life regression had occurred the previous day, when my sister had shown me a book on Egypt that she was buying as a gift for a friend. Flipping through the book, I had briefly seen an image of a king with an elaborate headdress. Now, standing on the cliff – still aching from the priestess's grief – I knew instinctively that the photo had been of the dead pharaoh I still mourned. The pharaoh turned out to be Akhenaton (I had channelled the name slightly wrong), and when I later researched the ancient kings of Egypt, my whole being responded as I read about him.

Never having experienced a regression of this kind, I was

astounded at how I had been transported – from one moment to the next – into the living experience of an unconscious memory! The only experience to which I could compare this, was the flashback I'd had of my Pleiadian playdate aboard the light ship. When I asked Amatron why my body had been bent backwards, he explained that I was being assisted in discharging old *miasms* – energetic blockages in my body. I had apparently just been healed of an old wound in my heart chakra.

He explained that *all* of the experiences I was having in the locations I was guided to visit – the Big Tree, Spitzkop and Coney Glen included – were assisting me in the release of miasms. This was one of the reasons I had been called back to South Africa; the "healing of the past" foretold by my guides involved not only my present-day family, but also the resolution of unhealed emotions from many lifetimes before.

The activations I was receiving were made possible by the potent vortices present in these power places, and my new guides were assisting in opening my energy body as much as possible in preparation for the global work that I would accomplish in the future.

When Amatron started using "we" and "us" instead of the first person, I realised that this was actually a collective of guides, like the Pleiadians. I didn't question Amatron's origin, but I registered that the two groups had very different purposes in connecting with me. Amatron was more scientific, teaching me about Earth energies, miasms in the body, and the postures and places that facilitate dimensional shifts. I was also being given information about past lives that were relevant to my present incarnation – as a Native American Indian, an Atlantean male elder; and a priestess in ancient Egypt.

Amatron told me that in my present lifetime my form had the potential to fully embody the united male and female – "the power and strength which the Tantras seek to achieve." The Amatron group had apparently worked with me in my Egyptian incarnation when I'd used similar forms of healing to those I was remembering in this lifetime. In ancient times there were restrictions placed on the knowledge that could be handed down to the masses, but we now live in a time where we have transcended those limitations. "Now is the time for *all* of humanity to be enlightened!" exclaimed Amatron.

In the days that followed I found it challenging to ground myself. The activations, new guides, and amount of information that I was being given were difficult to integrate. I was greatly assisted by following the guidance I'd been given in the original list of instructions; to call light to myself every day and to meditate under the stars every night.

Saying my final farewell to my mother was easier than I'd imagined it would be – she had made peace with her exit from the physical realm, happy to leave her painful body. Endings and beginnings often walk hand in hand. In this case, the death of my mother coincided with the ignition of a new path and identity for me, as a leader and awakener of the Light Tribe of Gaia.

View from Spitzkop

The last time I saw my mother

Having lunch with my sister

Witch doctor bones

Coney Glen Cave

Looking up into the canopy of the
'King Edward VII Big Tree'

CHAPTER 24

As Above, so Below

When I tried to explain the incredible experiences I'd had in Knysna to my London friends, they found it hard to conceal their incredulity. Even to my own ears it sounded like I'd been on an acid trip! As was my habit, I transcribed all the guidance I'd received word for word, in order to be able to look back at my nine-day journey and absorb what had transpired. What was as clear as day was that I was in for a dramatic acceleration of my path.

I had been instructed to teach two very new and different courses, *Awakening the Light Body* and *Channelling the Pleiadians*, but I had no idea how to approach the task. To my wonderment and joy, I discovered that I didn't have to figure it out on my own, for I had entered a phase in which I received very specific directions. "Ask and ye shall receive," proved to be an extraordinarily appropriate maxim with my new guides!

My first question was, *how* – in the conservative suburbs of South London – to attract students to these way-out Pleiadian courses. My previous approach to advertising had been to stick notices in local shop windows, and to leave leaflets in Balham Therapy Rooms where I worked. But the average Balham housewife was not particularly spiritually adventurous – meditation and yoga was usually as far as she ventured in the metaphysical world. When I asked the Pleiadians for assistance in magnetising participants to my new workshops, I was immediately shown exactly where and how to promote them.

In my inner vision I saw a woman opening her newly delivered *Cygnus* magazine, and an A5 turquoise leaflet falling out of it. The image was so clear that I even saw the photo of myself on the front page of the flier: dressed in purple, sitting cross-legged in a Namaste mudra, on the wooden deck in my garden! *Cygnus* is a metaphysical mail-order magazine with a wide distribution in the UK. I had never done "proper" advertising before and it was unbelievably cool to be shown exactly what to do! When I sat down to produce the flier, the precise layout and text was given to me, including the very same wording I'd received in the Knysna forest; an invitation to all those who wished to awaken, and to assist others to do the same.

When my leaflets were finally printed and distributed with the magazine, I received emails from the length and breadth of Britain from people who were connected to the Pleiadians, and thrilled to have a "Pleiadian Emissary" in the UK. By reaching out further into the world, I was attracting my soul family or *family of light*. I no longer felt alone!

My activations in South Africa enabled me to step forward confidently as a channel for the Star Councils of Light – the collectives of star beings that had elected to transmit through me to the people of Earth. They were also a massive opening for me on an energetic level; an initiation into my future path where I would work on a global level to reconnect the light grid at power places, both alone and as the leader of many different groups. When I had previously travelled to sites such as Stonehenge and Mount Shasta, I hadn't known how to tune into Earth energies. In Knysna, I learnt that this skill was not only easily within my grasp, but was also an avenue to healing and empowerment.

As part of my crash-course in energy training, my guides instructed that I travel in succession to several British sacred sites, some of them extremely remote. The most significant locales were to be visited at the important earth-sun conjunctions over the following six months. I was to be in Avebury for Beltane, Glastonbury for the Summer Solstice, the secluded island of Iona for Lammas, and Findhorn in the far northern reaches of Scotland for the Autumn Equinox. In these places I was to both charge my body and learn how to work with ley lines and energy vortices.

I was also asked to lead public ceremonies on the equinoxes and solstices, plus on the four Celtic "cross-quarter" dates of Imbolc, Beltane, Lammas and Samhain which mark the beginning of each season. I had already been following guidance to lead ceremonies in the yurt I'd built at the bottom of my garden, but I had never offered them out on the land in distant locations. It was an entirely new idea to get my head around, and a bit of a stretch out of my comfort zone.

My first mission was to lead a sunrise Beltane ritual on Silbury Hill, an ancient man-made ceremonial mound only a short walking distance from Avebury Stone Circle in Wiltshire. I was instructed to go a few days early in order to familiarise myself with the sacred landscape in its entirety, and to plan the ceremony. Four girlfriends had agreed to join me, and were due to arrive the night before Beltane at the campsite where I had set up my tent.

The sacred landscape includes the massive stone circle, two processional stone avenues that lead into the circle, the "Sanctuary" gathering place, Windmill Hill settlement, and several burial mounds or "long barrows."

A reconstruction of the stone circle & 2 avenues by the antiquarian Stukely.
Silbury Hill is in the foreground, the Sanctuary to the right.
Avebury Stone Circle is the largest in the world, over 1.3 km in circumference.
Each stone avenue is approximately 2.5 km long.

The agenda proposed by my guides started with a directive to spend an entire night alone up on Silbury Hill, which is known to be an energetic portal with a history of extraterrestrial activity. The assignment sounded exciting when I first received it, but at the time of my visit the hill was being restored and was strictly off-limits to the public. A barbed wire fence surrounded it on all sides and there were searchlights installed from two directions where the building huts and machinery had been placed.

On a cold and windy night with zero moonlight, approaching the hill through swampy terrain in order to be out of the radius of the lights, my assignment didn't feel fun at all. My guides had informed me that the authorities had in the past attempted to disconnect the inter-dimensional portal present there. That made me anxious about getting caught by these "authorities" in the act of illegally scaling the hill, but I was assured that I would be invisible to anyone not of the light. My experience on that night was very intense.

Having climbed over the barbed wire and clawed my way up the uneven rear side of the mound, pitted with rabbit holes, I was forced to settle on a slope in the wet grass in order to stay out of the lights. When I connected in with my guides, they said that I was there to be "de-coded," which was a new concept to me. They explained that aside from our twelve strands of DNA, which were in the process of being reconnected, the double helix in our DNA had been interfered with in order to limit our levels of awareness and memory. I was to trust that as I was de-coded overnight, memories and knowledge from Atlantis would awaken in me once more. At that point I was told in a very no-nonsense way to stop worrying, lie down and go to sleep.

For a light sleeper that seemed a very far-fetched idea, shivering in my damp sleeping bag on a bumpy hillside – but when I put my head down, I felt like I was knocked unconscious immediately. I was abruptly awoken just before dawn by a shrill internal alarm clock, literally repeating, "time to go, time to go" in a high-pitched drone. Not in need of further persuasion, I scrambled down the mound and hurried back to the safety and warmth of my B&B room for a well-deserved long, hot soak in the tub.

Over the following two days I traversed miles of countryside on foot, following exact instructions on the order that I should visit each location. The night up Silbury Hill and hours of marching through the countryside, sometimes in strong, cold winds, was lonely and physically challenging. I was so happy when my small gang of soul sisters duly arrived the night before the ceremony to keep me company. We sat around our campfire under the stars, drumming and singing, composing a special Beltane chant for the following day.

In the pre-dawn glow on the first of May 2007, we set off from the campsite, playing our drums and singing our chant as we proceeded down Beckhampton Avenue and into Avebury Stone Circle. Following in the footsteps of our ancestors, we continued through the dew-soaked grass down West Kennet Stone Avenue towards Silbury Hill. As the sun tried to peek through the grey clouds on the horizon, we climbed over the barbed wire and up to the top of the ceremonial mound. It felt much safer than it had in the dead of night, with the day-time construction crews still fast asleep. I led the *Seven Sacred Directions Meditation:** calling in the spirits of the North, South, West, East, all-that-is-above, all-that-is-below, finally leading us into the seventh direction, our own sacred hearts. It was a new experience for me, leading a ceremony out in the wild at sunrise, and I was aware that it was an initiation into my new work with Gaia which was of great significance.

As rewarding as the whole journey had been, it had also felt a bit like an endurance test. My next ceremony was to take place in Glastonbury at the Summer Solstice, and I asked the universe for more fun and more support from my tribe this time round. My call was answered in a pretty spectacular way!

The day before the event found me setting up my tent in a beautiful campsite on the outskirts of the famous Glastonbury tor. The tor is a natural hill that rises majestically from the flat plains called the "Somerset levels." It is topped with a dramatic stone tower, the only remnant of a medieval church and monastery. A dramatic landmark seeped in the myths of Camelot and the Holy Grail, the tor attracts thousands of pilgrims towards its energetic double-vortex.

In the campground I immediately made friends with a couple of guys in a nearby campervan. They entertained me with fascinating tales about the mystical land of Avalon, which exists in a parallel

---

* In this meditation you place 4 crystals to represent fire, water, earth and air around yourself, creating a 'Medicine Wheel' in which you are at the centre. See 'Free Meditations' on www.solara.org.uk.

dimension to the Glastonbury which you see from a third-dimensional perspective. I was already having fun and was thrilled when my new friends offered to show me the way to the top of the tor that evening.

I had once again been instructed to spend the entire night up on a sacred hill. This time, rather than being on my own, I discovered to my amazement that there were around two hundred people up there already, all with the same idea! Rather than shivering in sleeping bags, they were drumming, singing and generally partying the night away – staying awake in order to witness the solstice sunrise from this perfect vantage point.

The sound of the drums, chants and didgeridoo reverberated across the plains under the indigo night sky, evoking a timeless tribal atmosphere. Sunrise found me spontaneously leading a large crowd on the grassy banks in a solstice chant, drumming and singing my heart out. It was my first experience of leading a big group in a ceremony, this time with no prior planning, purely from the heart – and it felt wonderful!

I fell under the goddess spell of Avalon with its sacred red and white springs, Chalice Well gardens, the holy thorn tree seeded by Joseph of Arimathea, and the magnificent Glastonbury Abbey ruins. I also fell in love with the didgeridoo player from the tor celebration, manifesting the very same blonde-haired hippy about whom I had been fantasising in Knysna! Brendan was a Glastonbury aficionado, having considered it his spiritual home for many years, and he awoke me to its beauty and mystery. I was mesmerised by his knowledge, his didgeridoo playing and his connection with Avalon. I spent the following three days in a fairy-tale adventure with him in the land of mists, fairies and apple orchards, dragging myself back to London and my family responsibilities extremely reluctantly.

As I continued to journey to the power places of Great Britain, I realised how many people were already aware of the potent Earth energies in sacred sites. I was astounded at how asleep I had been in these matters over the years of my awakening. I had been studying spiritual books and practising techniques which were nearly all focussed in an upward direction. It was only after my journey in South Africa that I was able to relate to the potential of Gaia's energies to activate our own gifts.

The star collectives explained that each power place on our planet has its own personality. The ancestors who built the sites imbued them with their purpose, and every building or stone still holds the encoded memory of the rituals that have been performed there over thousands of years. I was given a vision of all the sacred sites across the planet reawakening, as higher dimensional energies stream down into the third dimension.

The sacred sites of Gaia are calling for our presence, so that we can assist in reconnecting them as inter-dimensional portals! Those of us who heed their call and assist in their reactivation, are reciprocally assisted in our *own* awakening.

I travelled with Brendan to many incredible sites over the following year, and together we were a living example of the old adage "As above, so below; as below so above." He was so connected with Earth energies that he could trace the path of ley lines that ran through the land without the aid of any tools. On the other hand, my intimate relationship with invisible higher-dimensional guides opened a whole new world to him. Between the two of us, we had skills that were to be invaluable in my *Gaia-and-Tribe* projects the following year.

I had come to a place where I perceived my life and path as an adventure with an unknown outcome, walking each step of my journey in wonder. My guides were ever-present, ready when called upon to advise me when I lost my way. I was morphing into a New-Age traveller, joyfully letting go of my old domestic life. My London garden was looking wild and the house wasn't as perfect as it used to be – but the children were thriving on the freedom I gave them, and all was well in my world.

Silbury Hill at dawn

The beautiful beech trees surrounding
Avebury

Nature spirits: a face & a fist in tree roots

In the gorgeous organic meditation cottage in Findhorn

On the sacred Isle of Iona   Amazing funnel clouds followed us

Walking the hills and beaches of Iona

PART 5

Warrior of the Light

CHAPTER 25

The Birth of Solara An-Ra

Nineteen fifty-eight, the year of my birth, must have been a "Gillian" year in South Africa. Of twenty girls in my senior year, four of us were Gillians: fully one-fifth of the class. "Gill" was the inevitable abbreviation, so I was rarely addressed by my christened name. The sound of my mother shouting "Gillian!" usually meant I was in trouble. Thus it was that I began this incarnation as "Gill Sheer." I always felt that my name was boring and didn't express who I truly was.

During my seven months in Iceland, aged twenty, I decided to call myself by my middle name, Eva – I felt it suited me better. I considered keeping this name permanently, but as soon as I returned to the States, there seemed to be no choice but to return to Gill – my friends were irrationally opposed to the idea of calling me by a new name. After getting married I decided to change my name to Gilly, using my new name, Gilly Colledge, as my professional therapist identity. But there were some close friends and family who insisted on continuing to call me Gill, much to my chagrin – I was amazed that changing one little letter could be met with so much resistance!

I assumed that Gilly Colledge would be my name for the rest of my life, but it's always a mistake to make assumptions. Many years later, in September 2007, I received a channelled message delivered by my friend Armukara Angel, in which her guides spoke of a major shift of energy that I would experience during my trip to Egypt the following year. Armukara had participated in one of my first *Opening to Channel* workshops, during which she had made a very strong connection with the Sirian Councils of Light. I trusted her channelling implicitly and always paid attention to messages she passed on, for our destinies were intertwined. The message from her guides read:

> Egypt will be a major shift for Gilly, and will change her. She will be given a new name, which she must

use, for this is who she will be from this point on.
She will change. People may not understand, but it
is the next stage of her path that she must take, and
she already knows this.

My initial reaction to the idea of being given a new name was
less than enthusiastic. I liked Gilly Colledge, and also had a wide client
base who knew me by that name. My previous experiences had indeed
proven that "people may not understand" if I chose to change my
identity. I also had reservations about the idea of taking on a spiritual
name, concerned that it might seem presumptuous unless I was given
one by a guru, as some devotees are. I let go of the idea for the
meantime, as my Egypt trip was still some months away.

Six weeks later, at a community celebration in Wales led by Roy
Littlesun, I asked a new friend, Urtema Dolphin, about her name.
Urtema is a powerful Goddess of a woman, and I was slightly in awe
of her. As I'd guessed, Urtema wasn't her original name, and I asked
what had inspired her to take on a new identity. "Oh, my guides just
started calling me Urtema," she said. She was so matter-of-fact and
confident about the process of taking on her true name, that over the
course of our conversation I let go of my fears about the impending
change and started looking forward to it. That opening manifested an
almost instant result. The very next morning, on the 28th of October
2007, I channelled a powerful Mayan elder spirit who pronounced in
a deep, authoritative voice:

> I am a warrior guide, a connector for you in the
> times to come in which your warrior status is
> revealed to all. You are one who awakens to your
> path indeed! Solara is your name – one who holds
> the power of the sun within her soul; within her
> words – the power of transformation. Yours is the
> way of power; the way of the warrior. Your way
> is one of impeccability and integrity. You are a
> *Warrior of the Light!* Your new name assists in the
> vibrational change to come.

When I shared the message with Urtema over breakfast, full of excitement, I said, "Well at least I like the name Solara, it's pretty – it would be difficult if I was given a name I didn't like." She burst out laughing. "Now, why on Earth would you take on a name that you didn't like – you do have some say in the matter you know!" Sometimes I do need to be told! She then proceeded to call me Solara for the rest of the weekend, which felt both strange and wonderful.

The following morning, in the early dawn, the Pleiadian Councils of Light commenced a transmission by singing, "Sooooo-laaaaa-raaaaa" three times. The vibration of the name echoed through my heart and soul, bringing tears to my eyes. This was an initiation into the vibration of SO-LA-RA, which was a higher frequency than I presently held. They explained that using the name and hearing myself called Solara would activate codes in my energy body and help me to integrate my Pleiadian Higher Self aspect.

On my return to London, I asked the universe for a very clear sign that this was indeed the new name of which Armukara's guides had spoken. My confusion was that it had been given before, rather than during, my journey to Egypt. The sign arrived a few days later when I met up with Urtema for a cuppa. "I've got something for you," she said with a mysterious smile while fishing in her bag. She told me that on her return from Wales she had started browsing through her books, pondering to herself, "Solara, Solara ... I know I've come across that name before."

After a dramatic pause at this point in her story, she pulled a white book out of her bag and placed it in my eager hands. Time stood still as I found myself staring at my new name in silver print with a rainbow sheen: SOLARA. The book was titled *The Star-Borne: A Remembrance for the Awakened Ones*, and the picture on the front was of a star radiating waves outwards like a radio signal.

As soon as I returned home I jumped onto my bed, preparing myself in a state of great anticipation to open the book for the first time. I closed my eyes and asked to be shown any significant message in it immediately. I then opened it at random, landing on page 82 – the start of a chapter explaining the purpose of taking on your

Higher Self name! The first words I read were:

> This name could be termed your multi-dimensional
> or starry name. And once received and used, the
> resonance of its vibration will serve to trigger and
> reactivate your pre-encoded cellular memories,
> allowing you to receive and harmonize with even
> higher frequency energy fields.

This was almost word for word what my guides had already explained about the purpose of my new name! To top it off, the author Solara went on to say that there are often a group of humans with the same "starry name," and that there were several Solaras. She mentioned having met another woman by the name of Solara in Sedona and being amazed at the similarities between them.

I was totally overwhelmed by this stupendous synchronicity. The universe had now given me a massively clear sign about changing my name that under no circumstances could be ignored. I found Solara's website and read about her in complete fascination. She was a beautiful, dark-haired American woman who had published many spiritual books long before I was ever awake. She had been a great leader in the Harmonic Convergence gatherings in 1987, and was one of the first people to talk of star gates. There was a picture on her website of her house in Hawaii, then for sale, and the way it was decorated looked so much like my house I was astounded!

I asked my guides if they could give me a second name, so I could distinguish myself from the other Solara in my work and future books. They said that if I wanted another name I should choose one myself. Easier said than done! Solara Colledge didn't work – it sounded too much like the name of an actual college – and why would I want to keep my married name anyway, when Jeremy and I had already been separated for three years? Solara Sheer sounded okay – but I couldn't imagine reverting to my maiden name either; it didn't feel right.

After much contemplation I chose *An-Ra*, in honour of the Pleiadian Archangelic collective by that name. According to Amorah

Quan-Yin, author of *The Pleiadian Workbook*, this collective is of a green frequency. As my incredible Pleiadian activation in Knysna had involved an intense turquoise-green light, I decided to honour the experience and my Pleiadian friends with this second name.

I went through the official procedure of applying for a "deed poll" to make my new name legal, which was surprisingly easy; followed by the much more long-winded process of changing every single document and account in my life. I was amused at having to pay an additional four pounds to change my title from "Mrs" to "Ms," rather than "Miss" – a tiny penalty imposed by the authorities for refusing to declare myself either married or single.

My approach towards any clients and friends who protested about the change was to be totally in my power about it. My guides were absolutely adamant that it was not an option for anyone to call me Gilly – it was no longer my name, and that was that. My children were massively supportive, respecting my wishes without question. This was no doubt helped by the fact that I was a popular mom with their gang of friends, who hung out at our house constantly – they thought my new identity was a cool eccentricity. Like Urtema, the teenagers accepted and used my new name immediately. As I drove down the neighbourhood streets, groups of kids would shout "Safe, Solara!" at me, knowing that it would make me giggle.

The strongest resistance to a name-change usually comes from close family. Shortly after changing to Solara, I went to a family birthday lunch with the children, and someone raised the subject. Predictably, a few people looked uncomfortable, and I was just thinking that I wouldn't force the issue, when thirteen-year-old Gabby piped up innocently, "I think it's rude for anyone to call mum by her old name when it's so important to her – it's just disrespectful not to call her Solara!" After a few seconds of stunned silence, my brother-in-law smiled and said, "Congratulations Solara, lovely name!" That was the end of the subject, and I have been called Solara by the whole family ever since. Out of the mouth of babes!

At the dawn of 2008 the Pleiadians said:

This name has come to you in order to activate your new path. This year, Solara An-Ra, Warrior of the Light, all flows in readiness for the plan. Your sword is illuminated, slicing through the veils, awakening all who come into contact with you on your path. Solara An-Ra, you pass the message on now from the Star Keepers of Knowledge. The time that has been appointed has come – a time of dedication; a time in which procrastination evaporates as the powers of the 'Higher Ones' are felt. Reconnect with your original intention. Step forth on your path of light!

At first I was puzzled by the term *Warrior of the Light*, as I had previously considered myself a *light worker* – and the term "warrior" had implications of "fighting against the dark" with which I didn't resonate. The P's explained that the most important quality of a warrior was *fearlessness*. Fear was the primary tool that had been used by the manipulators, and one of my gifts was to possess an in-built fearlessness in the face of all beings and programs that sought to disempower people.

The acceleration I experienced on my path once I took on my new name was phenomenal. I felt the energy of my Higher Self activating me every time I heard my name spoken! My life was different, and I was changing, as Armukara's guides had predicted. I was truly discovering the joy and empowerment that comes from stepping up to the mark and following the call of your true path.

CHAPTER 26

2012 Vision

As I visited a plethora of incredible power places in the UK over the course of 2007, my heart was opened to the profound mystery of the Sacred Isles. In Avebury and Glastonbury I had connected with what my guides called the "garden of England" in a way that I had never dreamt possible. Having loathed England during my early years in London, escaping to France for holidays whenever possible, I now found myself in love with this gentle green land. Avebury, in particular, drew me back again and again. My days spent exploring the rolling hills that formed voluptuous goddess sculptures in the landscape were always filled with magic.

On one trip, I walked back and forth across the fields for an hour trying to find Swallow Head Springs, a place considered holy by the same ancestors who had built the great stone circle. In my frustration I eventually shouted to the universe, "Show me where the spring is NOW please!" The thick bank of clouds parted instantaneously, an intense beam of light from the heavens illuminating one particular field. Laughing, I snapped a photo of the "finger of God" in the sky and ran towards the spot at which it was pointing. There it was – the sacred spring, bubbling out of Gaia in that very spot!

The same day I found myself magnetised into my first crop circle – a simple circle formed in perfect symmetry in a field of corn. I knew very little about crop circles, but was able to feel the light portal present within the exact circumference of the laid-down corn. I had of course read about the phenomenon prior to this, but it was my felt experience of the heightened energy in that field that sparked my fascination.

My boyfriend Brendan was gifted with what he called "future visions," in which he would spontaneously see a scene from an event yet to happen, like a future version of *déjà vu*. I had witnessed the manifestation of one of his visions when we were on the Isle of Iona.

Earlier, as we meditated together one morning in London, Brendan had described a scene in detail that included the two of us on a grey, stormy day on the edge of a windswept cliff. He couldn't tell where we might be or how far in the future it would be. A month later, out on the wild mountains of Iona wrapped up in waterproofs against the wind and rain, he suddenly grabbed my arm and exclaimed, "This is it! This is the scene I saw when we were meditating!" Goose bumps covered my body as I realised that I was wearing the pale blue hooded raincoat that he had seen in his vision, and that the setting of the rain, wind and blackened sky against the cliff were exactly as he had described.

Thus it was that when Brendan received two separate future visions of an important event I was to lead in 2012, I pricked up my ears! His first vision was of a large gathering around Avebury Stone Circle. Despite the fact that two busy roads cut through the circle as it now stands, there was no traffic present. He envisaged the whole group drawing in the potent earth energies within the stone circle, and redirecting and focussing them on a point in the sky where an inter-dimensional portal was opening. Brendan's second vision was of the energetic reactivation of Stonehenge, resulting in an outpouring transmission of energy to assist in the creation of the portal at Avebury.

Following these visions, I received a succession of urgent messages from the Star Councils of Light about an "Avebury healing project." The most significant of these messages was to come at the conclusion of a visit to Avebury at the Winter Solstice of 2007, where I had joined sound healer Gabriella Kapfer for a ceremony at West Kennet. I had been guided to walk around the whole circle, connecting my third eye with each stone still standing, and channelling where it felt appropriate.

At the stone that my guides had named "The Stone of Initiation" they said:

For you Solara, this is an initiation, which is a commitment towards the ceremony in 2012 which has been spoken of. And this is not a ceremony as you perceive it now – this is a particular energy exercise that awakens each one of those in the circle who stand on the embankment.

There is a Star of David to be activated in the British landscape – which aligns with Egypt, with South Africa and Table Mountain; with Peru and Machu Picchu; and with Palenque in Mexico. These places are to be activated and healed by you and all who are called to the mission. The purpose in Avebury is not only the healing of the stone circle – it is also to unite a band of light workers through love. Solara, you are called to unite bands of light workers through love and united purpose and intention.

This was the first of the assignments I'd been told about during my trip to South Africa, in which I was to attract a group of people in order to reactivate a specific power place. Unbeknownst to me, this first project had been initiated with the Beltane ceremony I had led on Silbury Hill earlier that year, and I had been preparing myself for it during all of my journeys to sacred sites. My work was to culminate at Beltane 2008, when crystals would be buried in the locations where the original stones were missing, to reconnect the flow in the circle.

I was simultaneously thrilled, excited and intimidated by the task I'd been given. Researching the history of Avebury Stone Circle, I discovered to my horror how much damage had been perpetrated in the early puritanical Christian era. The druid faith and druidic temples were considered a threat to the authority of the church leaders, who had gone to great lengths to destroy or remove most of the stones in the original circle. Some of the sacred megaliths, too huge to break up, had simply been toppled and buried where they fell. Despite the great work of restoration started by the antiquarian, William Stukeley, only 27 of the original 98 stones in the outer circle were standing, some of these having been unearthed and resurrected.

In my search for crystals that might be suitable for burying, I was offered 40 large, unpolished quartz points by a crystal and fossil retailer in Dorset. I wasn't sure, however, if they were the right crystals, how many were needed, or on which section of the stone circle I was to concentrate. Six weeks before Beltane, Brendan and I visited Avebury for the Spring Equinox with a very clear intention that all these questions would be answered, and everything came together in a beautiful way.

Our first step was to receive a dowsing lesson from Isabelle Kingston, a well-known and respected medium who had led healing work in the Avebury area for many years. She taught us how to use metal L-shaped rods, conventionally used for water dowsing, to establish the parameter of the aura of a standing stone. The edge of a stone's energy field was often several metres away from the stone itself – and, amazingly, the auras of the missing stones in the circle were just as easy to detect.

When I told Isabelle about our Beltane mission she suggested that, as the south-east quadrant of the circle was the one related to Beltane according to the "astrological clock," we might concentrate our efforts there. She said that she'd watched different groups doing healing in the circle for years, and that comparatively little work had been done in this quadrant because so many of the stones were missing. This instantly resonated. A flood of relief washed over me as I surveyed the quadrant in question – it suddenly made the project feel achievable!

The second part of the puzzle came together at the Red Lion Pub the following day, where five of us were having lunch. I was aware that amongst us there were three people; Brendan, Gabriella and Nina, who were all very tuned into Earth energies. Knowing that it was important to encourage other members of the group to make some of the decisions, I said to them, "I need to know if these 40 crystals I've been offered are the right ones. Can anyone help?" A silence descended on the table, and then all of the above-mentioned Earth-keepers started fiddling in their bags. When I realised that all three of them had their pendulums out and were tuning in to get an answer, a wonderful sense of anticipation arose in me. I watched the three swinging crystals responding to their silent questions, my excitement climaxing as they looked up and answered in a perfect trinity of confirmation: "Yes!" "Yes!" "Yes!"

On our last morning in Avebury, alone in the circle in the early dawn quiet, we decided to use the dowsing rods to answer the remaining questions about our work. Aside from their use in detecting the presence of water or energy fields, these metal rods can be used for *yes* and *no* answers in a similar way to a pendulum. Holding one or both rods so that they are balanced pointing directly ahead is the *neutral position*, from which they spontaneously move either in or out to indicate a yes or no response.

As Brendan had more skill than I with both pendulums and Earth energies, I acted as questioner while he held his rods in the neutral position, looking distinctly apprehensive about the responsibility I was laying on him. I fired a series of questions to which responses from the rods came with remarkable speed and clarity. Are we meant to be working in this south-east quadrant only? *Yes*. Are we to include the "inner circle" of stones in our work? *No*. Is 40 the right number of crystals to use? *No*. I knew instinctively then that it was a double number of crystals that was needed. Is 44 the right number? *Yes*.

At this point, having established that the crystals would be buried in this quadrant only, Brendan went to dowse the perimeter of the circle to establish the location of the missing stones. There are 2 massive stones on the western edge of that quadrant that had been numbered 1 and 98 by earlier researchers – the first and last, which comprise the entrance passage from West Kennet Stone Avenue. The whole of the remaining outer edge is bare of stones until the far eastern boundary, where there are two smaller stones lying down. Brendan noted a cross on a piece of paper each time he established where a stone had previously stood, counting 20 crosses in total.

We looked at a map of the circle I'd picked up at the village museum, and noticed for the first time that the two final stones on the eastern edge were numbered 76 and 77. We looked at each other. 77 plus 20 equals 97 – which would make the following stone number 98.

The next standing stone was 98! A huge grin appeared on Brendan's face, and I let out a massive *"WHOOHOO,"* as we danced a jig in celebration. We had only just learnt to use the rods the day before, so it was thrilling to have this new skill confirmed so definitively. If we had noticed the numbers on the map beforehand, we could have avoided playing detective and worked out through simple arithmetic that there were 20 missing stones – but this way we knew that Brendan had the skill to pinpoint the exact location where the crystals were to be buried when the big day arrived!

Brendan suggested that we might bury two crystals in the location of each missing stone, one pointing up and one down, to hold the energy of the masculine and feminine. That would account for 40 crystals – but why had the number we needed just been established as 44? We looked around, ruminating about this last piece of the puzzle. I asked Brendan, "What about the small area of land to the east of stone 76?" He dowsed this area and low and behold – the energy of missing stones numbered 74 and 75 showed themselves immediately through the rods. The picture was complete – 22 missing stones for our 44 crystals!

I had one last task to complete before leaving Avebury: the burial of a large quartz point which I had owned for many years. This crystal had communicated to me that it would serve the purpose of sending energy from the top of Silbury Hill to the stone circle when our work was complete.

The sight that greeted me at the top of the hill was very different from three months earlier at the winter solstice. Instead of a gaping hole where the centre of the mound had collapsed, there was a pond of chalk-slush that was only partially set. The National Trust was back-filling the hole with a chalk composite in order to stabilise the structure.

There was still a huge fence barricading the hole, with the addition of a camera trained on the middle – presumably to keep track of how the composite settled as it solidified. I slithered on my belly under a gap in the fence, smearing myself with chalk from head to toe in the process. Crouching on the edge, I positioned myself where I hoped the camera couldn't spot me. I directed my prayers into the crystal – for both the healing of Silbury Hill and for the blessing of our Avebury mission – and placed it in the grey-white sludge. It descended slowly until just the tip of the point was visible, and then stopped, glinting in the sunlight, frozen forever in its sacred resting place.

I channelled a beautiful message from the Pleiadians:

> Your intentions, dear children, are what allow you to real-ise the energy and power of this project. There will be an activation within the group, so that the result will be the healing and awakening of the people within the group. As your purpose to assist the Earth is manifested, so Gaia's inner purpose is real-ised – to raise your vibrations, dear children. As your love for Gaia flows into her through your clear and high intentions, so the healing flows into your cellular matrix – and the reawakening of your ancient powers is manifest.

Channelling at the 'Stone of Initiation'   The 'Finger of God' pointing at Swallow
Head Spring

In my first corn crop circle

The partly restored NW quadrant of Avebury circle, surrounded by the 'henge' or
embankment. Small concrete posts indicate where stones once stood. Avebury Village,
which you see in the distance, now sits in the centre of the circle.

CHAPTER 27

Gaia-and-Tribe Reconnection

When, in preparation for the project, I visited the Avebury circle over the next few months, I discovered something that amazed me. Some of the individual massive standing stones were functioning as extraterrestrial portals! At one of these stones I made contact with the captain of an Andromedan spaceship, who informed me that he and his group were observing the earth's progress from that station. When I asked if he was a new guide, he laughed and replied in the negative – I had simply tuned into him because I had asked to connect with the highest energy possible while in that portal – and he had happened to be there!

In March 2008, exactly a year after my Pleiadian activation in South Africa, I found myself connecting with a Sirian collective at a huge portal stone in the southern inner circle. I was sheltering from a crazy snow storm that had appeared out of nowhere, a strong wind blowing a sheet of fluffy snowflakes directly from the east. As I pressed against the western side of the ancient megalith, which was about four metres in both height and width, I spontaneously shifted into a very high state of consciousness. Switching my recorder on, I channelled this message:

> Blessed light being of the earth plane, we greet you in synchronous harmony and time. We are beings of the *Elakon Order of Melchizedek*, from Sirius. We light beings work with you now, Solara An-Ra, if you so choose. You will choose for the highest good of all, from your heart, understanding that the connection of the extraterrestrial with the human is a power point – a starting point for many things.

"No kidding!" I laughed to myself.

The time had come for me to put the information for the

Avebury Healing Project up on my website. In a newsletter, I requested that anyone who wished to be a part of the mission step forward. A group of excited volunteers soon gathered, and at our first meeting we made an affirmation to cement our intention: "The energy and power of Avebury's sacred circle is restored, according to the *Divine Plan for Ascension on Gaia.*"

My guides instructed me to record a new meditation and to make the sound file available for download on my website. They called the meditation *Essential Daily Practices**, stating that its purpose was to keep the vibration of all participants as high as possible in the lead-up to the event. They added that hundreds of thousands of people across the world would come to practise this and other recordings that I would make freely available to the world. I found that hard to believe, as my outreach was hardly global at that time – but it surely came to pass, largely due to the extremely practical and enjoyable nature of the guided meditations gifted through the Star Councils of Light.

When I unpacked the 44 clear quartz crystals I'd ordered, I was thrilled to discover that in their unpolished state they had a beautiful rose tinge to them. As a surprise gift, my supplier had included one extra crystal, a much larger transparent quartz point. My guides instantly named this the "connector crystal," saying that it was to be buried at Windmill Hill, outside of the circle, the morning after the initial project. Its role was apparently to help stabilise the re-connection of energies within the stone circle that we would achieve. In every twist and turn of the project there was magic afoot!

The group of volunteers consisted largely of London people, most of whom had little experience of working with Earth energies. We went through several stages after receiving the crystals, the first being to bury them in the soil of my friend Philly's vegetable allotment. Our intention was to neutralise them before charging them for their new purpose, but we were delighted to hear from the

---

* There are 3 versions of this meditation free to download on my site: an 8-minute, 13-minute and 10-minute 'new' version created at a later date. The meditation is unusual in that it contains a series of invocations, to be spoken out loud – but is the most effective practice I have ever used to centre, clear, ground and protect myself on a daily basis.

guides afterwards that the allotment land had received healing from the crystals in the process. We did our work at the crack of dawn, surrounded by the early morning chorus of birdsong, and dug them up five days later for the first of several group meetings where the crystals were charged and dedicated for their purpose.

At the meetings many people were blown away by the fact that the crystals "communicated" with them. We could feel their energy so powerfully; and, as we poured love into them, we in turn were charged, because of the amplification powers inherent in quartz crystal.

My guides told us:

> The Goddess Gaia brings forth fruit from the seeds in her belly. She gifts crystals only in order that they may be used, and this these crystals know – that they are being put to good use, rather than being admired as objects. Crystals wish to be used if extracted from the belly of Gaia. This must be stressed – they must be used consciously, and communicated with; cleansed and charged, in order for the sacrifice of being ripped from the belly of the Mother to be justified.

They spoke further on the concept of Earth healing, explaining that Gaia was in fact always able to heal herself if she chose. They explained that the "rippling of her skin," which was happening in the form of earthquakes all over the world, was indeed one of her ways to self-heal. Once again they reiterated that what we were doing would result in a two-way reconnection – in both the energies of the stone circle and in the people who were involved – and asked me to therefore re-name the project "Gaia-and-Tribe Reconnection." Thus were a great series of *Reconnection Projects* birthed in my life!

The long-awaited Beltane weekend finally arrived, and everything fell into place beautifully. Brendan and I went down a day early to spend time in the first crop circle of the season – a rapeseed glyph depicting six crescent moons, located beside Silbury Hill. Meditating in the centre, I received information from my new Sirian guides that gave me goose bumps. They said that a new circle would appear directly after our work was complete, symbolising what we had achieved.

Our work began at Swallow Head Springs where we were guided to bury a large rose quartz, gifted by Urtema, who had joined us in this work. As the group gathered for the first time in our opening ceremony, the enthusiasm was infectious. The gentle energy of the holy spring and the clear flowing waters of the Kennet River where we sat opened our hearts, cleansed and grounded us. The number of people participating had fluctuated the week before as some joined and others cancelled at the last moment. My guides had said that there would be 22 of us, perfectly coordinated with the 22 pairs of crystals that would be buried, and so it was.

That night, in the eerie midnight darkness of the ancient stone circle, we gathered between the entrance portal stones. We had chosen to do the work at night so as to avoid attracting attention to ourselves, as I had been warned that the National Trust would never give permission for our work. I had also had some disapproval directed my way regarding the idea of tampering with the soil in a protected historical landmark, but had overcome any doubts, trusting that – as our affirmation stated – what we were doing was in line with the Divine Plan for Gaia. Brendan had devised a method of burying the crystals using a bulb-planting tool, so as to cause minimum disturbance of the soil. When the crystals were in position, the soil and grass could be replaced with perfect precision.

As each person sat in the seat of the Stone of Initiation, I smudged them with white sage. Urtema then anointed the two crystals they held with her precious alchemical combination of "World Waters," from Swallow Head Spring, the Red and White Springs of Glastonbury and multiple other sacred sites around the world. At this point each crystal was connected to the etheric grid of the entire circle. Wrapped up in blankets against the cold, we then moved from marker to marker around the perimeter of the circle, burying each pair of crystals with an invocation of love to Mother Earth. The atmosphere was electric with excitement as we literally felt portals of light opening and reconnecting around the circle!

Each one of us was in awe of the enormity and beauty of the task we had taken on – like the priests and priestesses of Atlantis, we were working with crystals and Earth energies to reconnect Gaia's light grid and assist our human tribe's evolution. Just as my guides had predicted, when I scouted the goddess hills near our B&B the following morning, there was a brand new crop circle – a perfect triple-moon laid down in rapeseed beneath the Alton Barnes White Horse. The design fitted in perfectly with the theme of the Mother-Father-Child trinity that had emerged during the project – an amazing confirmation from the star beings that we had succeeded in our task.

It had started raining by the time we spotted it, but nothing was going to stop me from entering. Sitting in the central circle of the glyph I did some alternate nostril breathing, and everything went perfectly still. Suddenly a blue-white current of electricity shot through my whole body, directly followed by a spectacular vision of how the central circle was laid down. In the flash-back I saw the rapeseed plants being blown down in a perfect swirl by a beam of light-sound emanating from a Sirian light ship. When I opened my eyes, I was staring at the crops in the exact swirl that I'd just seen – a twisted centre point of three plants remaining vertical, creating a perfect geometric "dot" in the pattern when seen from above. Each delicate plant stalk was bent over with absolute precision, without a single stem broken! It is one thing to read theories of how crop circles are made, and another to experience an actual replay!

My Sirian guides told me that I had received yet another activation, and that this would aid me with several "letting-gos" which were necessary in my personal life. As they said this, my first thought was of Brendan, waiting for me outside of the circle. Over the previous few months we had struggled to keep our long-distance relationship together, the intensity of the project being one of many factors that had caused tension between us. Brendan thought that I relied too much on my guides and was starting to lose touch with the "real world" – while I knew that the guidance I was receiving was a gift in every way.

Our relationship was indeed the first letting-go, and the break-up was painful. I was on my own again, unwillingly so, but I understood that in the years leading toward 2012 my priority must be my chosen mission to assist Gaia and my human tribe.

The 44 quartz crystals, just unpacked

About to be buried in Philly's allotment

Drumming up the energies at Swallow Head Springs

Over-excited & rain-drenched, in front of the triple-moon circle

Drumming around the Beltane fire

Our Beltane celebration the evening after the project: Armukara & Dana to my right

CHAPTER 28

Naked into the Wild

In preparation for my first trip to the temples of Egypt in June 2008, I decided to do a vision quest. This is an ancient shamanic tradition, often undertaken at times of transition, in which you spend some days out in nature, in isolation, in order to receive guidance or "visions" from the ancestors and Mother Earth. The preparation phase takes place at the base camp with the leader and other participants.

This is followed by the quest itself; several days and nights during which you walk away from everyday life and spend time with only Mother Earth and her creatures as your companions. One of the essential principles of the journey is to do without food, books, music or stimuli of any kind that might distract you. In the final stage you come back to base camp for an integration period in which you are reunited with the group – a time to share any visions or guidance you might have received.

After some research I found a vision quest being hosted by an elder woman shaman on a very large, beautiful farm north of Penzance in Cornwall. It included a four-day period out on your own, with three days of preparation beforehand and two days of integration at the end. Four days and nights without any food and limited water sounded like a massive challenge, but I knew it would help with the energetic clearing that I needed before the big shift I was to undergo in Egypt.

Several weeks later found me at the base camp in Cornwall, sitting around the fire listening to the stories of the other participants. I realised that the guidance I received on an everyday level meant that I was living in a different reality from the people I was with. Over the three preparation days I found myself resisting the advice on how to handle the impending period of solitude – I wanted the spirits of Gaia and nature to be my teachers. When the big morning dawned I was ecstatic that the adventure was beginning!

I was happy to leave my everyday crutches behind: computer, phone, diary, makeup, cosmetics, watch, jewellery, music and camera. I even opted for the no-toilet paper option, choosing to use leaves instead. My greatest challenge was to do without my precious tape recorder. I always recorded my channelling in order to retain the guidance – and surely important messages would be given during this time? I left it behind reluctantly, in the spirit of going "naked into the wild" as our ancestors had done.

My provisions for the four days consisted of bedroll, sleeping bag, a tiny one-man tent, one change of clothes, rain poncho, sharp knife, insect repellent, lip salve, sunscreen, torch, rattle, journal, pen, hand-spade for burying toilet waste, and two litres of water. The torch was to be used only for emergencies; the natural light of the stars and first-quarter moon was sufficient to illuminate the hours of darkness.

After being blessed and smudged by our shaman at daybreak, we set off for the piece of land we had each carefully chosen the day before. The area I had opted for was a beautiful field of wild bluebells, cow parsley, bracken and grasses; high enough to have views over the valley and surrounding hills. To begin the process of making my sacred space, I had been instructed to measure out a circle roughly nine metres in diameter. This circle was to be my home for the next four days and nights, as there was no walking about on this type of vision quest.

The first step involved finding rocks or stones to place around the perimeter of the medicine wheel, representing the eight directions. I thanked and smudged each rock with white sage, offering a prayer to the spirits of each direction. Two further "circles of beauty and strength" were created as I sprinkled first tobacco, and then corn flour, in concentric rings around the stones for protection.

Being a compulsive home-maker, I amused myself by making my new abode into different living areas. Within my circle I had a bedroom in the form of my tent, a bathroom area behind a gorse bush (that doubled as a place to shelter from strong winds), a flat rock near the centre for meditation, and a groundsheet in a clear space for exercise and resting. The crowning glory of my camp – and the reason I had chosen this particular spot – was a handsome big rock in the north on which I planned to sing and rattle as the sun set over the distant sea.

With my space dedicated, blessed and organised, I decided to celebrate by lying naked in the sunshine on my groundsheet. Blissed out in the midday sun and cool breeze, I drifted off, waking up a couple of hours later to a terrifying sound – like the snorting of an angry dragon! When I dared raise my head I was presented with the vision of a large black bull, staring straight at me with bloodshot eyes, snorting loudly through streaming nostrils! Recalling stories I'd heard of bulls chasing strangers out of their fields, I lay there frozen in terror. Unsure whether it would be better to stand up and challenge the creature or be submissive, I tried mentally willing the beast to go away. Instead he moved closer, stepping right into my sacred circle, and I scrabbled to my feet in horror. Picking up my rattle I backed slowly towards my large rock, shaking it as loud as I could.

Earlier in the day I had sung to the plants, birds and rocks, asking them to support me. Now, stark naked on my rock, I sang my story to the bull, telling him of my mission and asking him to go on his way peacefully. As suddenly as he had appeared, he turned and started walking away. A few meters from my camp he stopped, craning his head around for one final look at me – and I swear that for a moment his blank expression showed the hint of an amused smile. Having grown up in the city, I had very little experience of farm animals. I hadn't registered that the bull in fact had no horns, and was therefore a cow – a friendly old cow with a bad cold, I found out afterwards from the farmer!

The sun was now heading for the horizon, and a feeling of panic set in about the total absence of food, people and entertainment. I was on an idyllic desert island with no coconuts or Robinson Crusoe. Casting around for something to do, I remembered that I was supposed to repair my circle if it had been disturbed, using the tobacco and corn I'd kept in reserve. As I sprinkled the tobacco over the part where the cow had entered, I suddenly realised that I was holding in my hand a potential vice – I actually had some loose tobacco! I had never been a cigarette smoker, but had picked up the habit of occasionally having a puff on Brendan's roll-ups. The idea of an illegal ciggy was suddenly irresistible.

I tore a little rectangle off a corner of a page in my journal – my only source of paper – and made a roll-up by sticking the edges together with peppermint lip salve. Genius! Triumphantly wielding my decadent smoke, I sat watching the sun being sucked into the distant ocean. Three puffs later I was overcome by violent nausea and had to go lie down in the tent. I laughed at the absurdity of what I'd just done, which started an irrepressible giggling fit. "Oh my Goddess," I thought, "only one day out here and I'm laughing like a crazy woman, singing to bulls and smoking lip salve – what am I going to be like at the end!"

When I recovered, I sat outside in the rapidly fading light to ask for guidance. At the time I considered writing-channelling to be less powerful than the direct-voice method, but in the absence of my tape recorder I had no choice but to try it. Indeed, this was one of the gifts of the quest – realising that channelling in this form was just as useful and accurate. I connected straight away with Elakon, who said:

> The immediacy of your predicament is in the hearts and minds of many, dear Solara. On the one hand, you are ready to hold the codes – and on the other, your complacency holds you back from achieving all that you might at this crucial time. Hold fast to your course Solara An-Ra. Do not look left or right, or distract yourself with childish needs and Earth-bound trivialities.

I was being told off for obsessing about my break-up with Brendan and indulging in meaningless addictions, but as ever the tone was loving and wise. As I sat on my meditation rock, wondering why my Sirian guides were temporarily more dominant than the Pleiadians, I received the response:

> Never fear that your Pleiadian connection is lost dear child. We are here for you night and day,

lighting the way and bringing blessings. We come to you in your sleep, when you are not aware, and gift you with our tales and codes, assisting you with this shift our Sirian brothers speak of.

This brought tears of gratitude to my eyes.

I was surprised that by the end of the second day I had already stopped thinking about food. More of an issue were the hours of darkness, where I tossed and turned all night on the cold hard ground. My dreams were obscure and confusing, and I grew increasingly frustrated about the lack of "visions" that I was receiving. On the days when the sun shone I tried to meditate, but I found concentration difficult and turned to writing in my journal instead.

On the third day, feeling extremely spaced out, I decided to try a shamanic journey. It was my most successful attempt yet, assisted no doubt by having fasted for so long. Sitting on the earth, beating my rattle in a steady rhythm, I was amazed by how quickly I entered an altered state. After only a matter of minutes I was given a vision of a young Native American squaw, paddling along a river in a small wooden canoe. The experience was like being in a lucid dream, slipping between being the girl and watching her. She was crying as she rowed, tears streaming into her long black hair, a great dilemma burning in her heart. Secretly in love with a young man from an enemy tribe, the decision she faced was whether to follow her heart and run away with him, or to stay with her tribe and be heartbroken.

After being shown the situation, I asked Great Spirit what the right choice would be. Surely to be true to herself she would have to go with her beloved, for that was where her heart lay? The reply was:

No, the right decision would be to stay with her tribe – for if she left, her unfulfilled roles within the tribe would always leave a hollow in her heart. Whereas in the tribe, she would eventually partner another, have children, and play all the roles that were part of her tribe and ancestry. The memory of her first love would transmute from the initial heartbreak into a pleasant secret of her passion for a handsome young man in her youth.

Time, as it so often does, would heal the wound.

Thus was the vision given to me on my quest. I had made the "other" decision over and over again in my life. Feeling unsupported by my original tribe, I had chosen always to place my "true love" first, even when that love turned out not to be true. Lying on my back in the field of wild grasses and flowers, I reflected on the relationships that had dictated my life – and on the resolve I'd made at the completion of the Avebury Gaia-and-Tribe project. The time had come for me to put my light tribe first.

My trip to Egypt was the first step; a preparation for my work to come. As the thought caused an uncomfortable shiver to run down my spine, I heard my guides say: "We are with you star child – we are with you always."

CHAPTER 29

Initiation in the Land of Khem

Immediately after my first trip to Egypt, my newsletter read: "What happened to the days when I went on normal holidays – swimming in the sea, reading a novel, chilling out at sunset with a glass of *rosé* and a lover? These days I travel on my own to unlikely places, a hint of danger often involved, and have weird experiences! Challenges, it seems, are often spiritual shortcuts, bringing in their wake the progress that we seek on our paths."

Egypt was a big-time challenge. It started before I even got on the plane, with warnings from my guides so different from their usual communications that it was hard not to feel nervous. The day before I left they asked me to proclaim the following:

> I, Solara An-Ra, invoke the presence of the almighty sword of Michael! My aura-shield protects me at all times from all manipulation. I, mighty warrior of Ra, announce my presence in the lands of Ra, the Gods at my side as friends and allies, united against all foes.

They seemed to be preparing me for the onslaught of enemies!

From the minute I stepped onto Egyptian soil, I felt overwhelmed. The Egyptian summer was much too hot for me, resulting in my being laid low with sunstroke after only two days in the country. Even worse than the heat was the continual harassment – for money, sex, taxis, camel rides, tours, trinkets – it was relentless. A grinding chorus of "Hey lady, where you from lady?" followed me incessantly. It was incomprehensible to me that a taxi driver would propose marriage only ten minutes into a conversation. Were there really women out there who responded to such clumsy advances?

I had been guided to go on my own and with no set agenda, having been given assurance that I would be supported on my journey through the temples of the Nile. I assumed that my helpers would be fellow travellers, as had been the case in India, but my primary aids turned out to be the Gods and Goddesses of ancient Egypt. These deities have safe-guarded the temples of the Nile for centuries, and are still present as energies that can be channelled.

I was also assisted by the Egyptian temple guards who, despite the fact that there was invariably a *baksheesh* or tip involved, aided me greatly on several occasions. The first of these was in Luxor temple, which I entered one early dawn in order to escape a horde of ferry, taxi and carriage owners who were fighting over how I would get to Karnak temple. Once the guard understood that I wanted to meditate, he took me to a quiet spot where I could rest undisturbed. Before he left me he placed my hand on a five-pointed star on the carved temple wall, afterwards bringing it to my third eye, and finally to my heart. Left on my own, I sank immediately into the first moment of peace since my arrival.

After the familiar nodding of my head that I had come to expect when my guides connected in, my posture was adjusted and my breath was forcibly expelled from my lungs. In this "frozen" physical position, ribcage expanded, I entered a spontaneous breathless state – no inhalation or exhalation whatsoever. I had read about the breathless state of Samadhi, but had never experienced it. It was confusing at first to feel as if I'd left my body – I didn't appreciate the "bliss of union" because my expectation was to receive guidance rather than to go into the void. My guides were in fact blessing me with an awesome teaching, but my trip was long past by the time I appreciated what had been gifted.*

As my journey through the temples continued, I kept being catapulted back into a state of fear and vulnerability. In the inner sanctuary of Horus of the Seti temple, I felt dark energies gathering around me, which made the hairs on the back of my neck stand up. Thoth came to me in my meditation and said:

---

* The breathless state, aside from taking one into the 'union with the Divine,' allows one to experience the body as simply light or energy, and one with everything else in creation. It is therefore a fantastic preparation in our ascension process, for activating the light body, helping us to activate our higher-dimensional powers and experiencing unity consciousness.

In these temples where darkness resides, it
is necessary to call the light in. Visualise the
octahedron now (a four-sided pyramid with a
mirror image pointing down) – carry this with you
as a protective emblem, and hold it to ignite within
you a connection from above and below.

I was told repeatedly before, during and after Egypt that I
was being "coded" in order to reactivate the memory of my stellar
heritage and powers. I was also apparently "announcing my presence
to the energies of the land" in the various temples, in preparation for
my entry into the Great Pyramid at the end of the trip. I had to learn
not to give away my power to any energy, person or obstacle along
the way. I was reminded that I was in training to be an invincible and
fearless light warrior, not only in the safety of my home in London,
but in every circumstance – able to be in a state of peace in the eye
of the hurricane.

There was occasionally a break in the clouds where things flowed
smoothly, one of these welcome interludes taking place in Karnak. I
sailed to the enormous temple complex in a Felucca boat early one
morning, enjoying the splendour of the sunrise on the tranquil Nile.
Fighting my way through a sea of tourists I managed to locate what
I'd come to see – the small inner chamber of the Ptah temple where
a life-sized granite statue of Sekhmet still stood intact. An angel in
the form of a temple guard materialised just as I found it. Not only
did he light three candles for me in front of the statue, he allowed me
to meditate on my own for about twenty minutes while he barred the
door from intruders.

The Sekhmet statue came alive in the flickering candle light,
electrifying me with her piercing lion eyes – but with such love
radiating from her presence, I felt like I was melting. She asked me
to look into the darkness of my soul, in order to let go of the veil
of illusion. In the photos I took of Sekhmet, the orbs are so profuse
they almost obscure the statue completely.

My journeys between the various temples tended to be
challenging, interspersed with short but intense intervals in the temples

themselves that were fascinating and rewarding. In the temple of Isis, both Isis and Osiris taught me about dignity and dedication. In the temple of Hatshepsut I connected with the amazing, loving energy of the Hathors – an ascended civilization who worked through the cult of the Goddess Hathor in ancient Egypt.

My final three days took me to Saqqara and the Giza plateau. The whole trip had been leading up to this final destination and I couldn't help feeling anxious that it would be a let-down, or that I wouldn't fulfil the mission that my guides had hinted at in the Kings Chamber. My first attempt to enter the Great Pyramid was very frustrating. Having gotten up at the crack of dawn in order to be first in queue and avoid the heat of the sun, I discovered that the ticket only allowed me entry onto the plateau. To get the actual entry pass I had to walk right across to the other side of the pyramids where the tourist buses were already parked. I ran all the way there, sweating profusely, but by the time I got to the front of the queue, the maximum quota for that day was already filled.

As I stomped off, back down the hot dusty road, stressing about my chances of getting into the pyramid at all, a camel driver started the usual spiel. "Ride a camel lady?" No, thank you. "Camel ride very nice, ride a camel lady?" No reply. "Where you from lady? You from Germany?" Leave me alone please. "You married lady? You want a husband?"

At this point I totally lost the plot; the accumulation of all the hustling, the heat and the vulnerability of being on my own finally taking its toll. I started screaming like a lunatic, swearing in an extremely unspiritual manner. "If you don't f*ck off and leave me alone I'll report you and your bloody camel for harassment! Say ONE more f*ing word and I'll get you locked up!"

I was shouting so loudly that tourists started to gather around in fascination, which then attracted two tourist police. "There is a problem, lady?" I was on a roll, all the frustration of the previous eight days exploding from me. "Yes there f*ing is!!! I have been hassled for eight solid days by camel owners, shop keepers and taxi drivers! If this man refuses to leave me alone, I insist that he is arrested! I would like to walk back to my hotel without another f*ing word from anyone!"

To their credit, the policemen knew when it was wise to support a crazy foreign lady. Without a word of admonishment, they gently escorted me away from the scene of the crime and right to the door of my hotel. Obeying my explicit instructions they did this in total silence, simply bowing slightly with bemused smiles as they left me. I closed the door of my bedroom and burst out laughing.

The universe sent me another blessing that night, in the form of a very entertaining evening with the since deceased Abd'el Hakim Awyan, known by many as the "holy man" of Giza. I had been trying to contact him for days with no success, but when I came down for dinner on this occasion he was sitting right outside his house on the pavement, as if I was an old friend he was waiting for.

Abd'el was an absolute character and rebel, puffing away on his hashish pipe while telling stories of his lifetime on the Giza plateau, and the mythologies that are at the heart of ancient Egyptian wisdom. He drew me a picture of the Goddess Nut, explaining her role in universe; and she visited me in my dreams that night, assuring me that all would be well on the morrow.

Sure enough, I had no problem gaining entrance to the Great Pyramid the following morning, and soon found myself ascending a narrow sloping passageway behind a steady stream of tourists. After a short while in the Queen's Chamber, I continued up, finally entering the famous King's Chamber. It was difficult not to feel a bit of anticlimax after all the stunningly painted and decorated temples I had visited. Here was a square room made of large greyish stone blocks, dank and a bit claustrophobic. The stone sarcophagus was likewise unprepossessing in appearance.

In order to avoid a tourist jam, the guard on duty kept us moving forward; much to my distress, we were not allowed to meditate or linger too long in the room. I urgently called on my guides and angels to help me achieve whatever I was meant to be accomplishing. The next minute there was some shouting from the stairwell outside, and the guard left to see what was going on. I slipped down to the floor on the far side of the sarcophagus, back against the cool stone wall, and tuned in. A few minutes into my meditation I felt a sudden stillness and quiet in the room. Miraculously, the King's Chamber, which had been buzzing with tourists only moments before, was totally empty! Without a second's hesitation I jumped over the low wall and lay down in the sarcophagus.

The minute my head hit the stone base, my third eye opened front and back as a line of brilliant light shot through my head. I had heard that the sarcophagus was used by initiates as an inter-dimensional portal, and I was indeed aware of a higher dimension accessible to me if I chose to travel along the pathway of light. But I knew that this was not my present purpose in the pyramid. I was simply accessing a memory of a time when I had lain in this very tomb – a time when I remembered how to travel inter-dimensionally in my light body. This memory was necessary for the re-coding I was receiving in Egypt.

When the guard returned, shouting vehemently in Egyptian, I snapped back into the present time. I opened my eyes as he looked down at me, and there was a moment where his feigned look of horror melted. We smiled at each other, mutually acknowledging my right to be exactly where I was, regardless of the rules. He helped me up and over the wall again as I slipped him the expected baksheesh, and the next minute the chamber was full of tourists and bustle again. What had just happened seemed utterly impossible to imagine.

On my last morning I meditated on the roof of the Sphinx Guest House at sunrise, staring into the eyes of the sphinx. The final words from my guides were:

> The land of Khem bids you farewell. Your presence
> in this land has affected the energies here – believe
> this to be so! The opening of your heart has made
> this more accessible for each one who journeys
> here – whether on a sacred quest or no. Know that
> your heart is energetically connected with the heart
> of the Sphinx now – and it is so.

They also announced that I would return to Egypt as the leader of a group, and that I would be totally supported on that journey. This first trip had apparently served as preparation for the second, which would be joyful and powerful for all concerned. The last ten days had felt so challenging that it was hard for me to imagine wanting to return, and my guides were well aware of that. "We'll see about that!" was my response to their announcement. For a change, my star friends were silent – but I felt their amusement and loving presence, as always.

The pyramids from my room in the Sphinx Guest House

The 5-pointed star in Luxor Temple

Sekhmet obscured by orbs

With the 'holy man of Giza,' Abd'el Hakim Awyan

PART 6
Reconnecting the Codes

CHAPTER 30
Crop Circle Crazy

2008 and '09 can officially be declared my years as a "croppie." My preoccupation with crop circles was sudden and intense, springboarded by my incredible experience in the 2008 triple-moon glyph near the Alton Barnes White Horse.* During this encounter, my Sirian guides gave me a crystal clear play-back vision of how the circle had been imprinted into the field – through a light-sound frequency that interacted with the earth's electromagnetic field. Witnessing the spectacular pattern in the rapeseed field first-hand, immediately after that vision, will forever be imprinted into my memory.

I was amazed that I had lived in London for so long oblivious to the fact that the most famous area in the world for this phenomenon was right on my doorstep. My investigation into the science behind crop circles convinced me that it was *the* breaking news of the century – and yet the general public, ever sheep-like, had bought into the ludicrous "rope-and-plank" theory of circle production promoted in a couple of scam TV broadcasts. Some circles are undoubtedly man-made, but there is hard-core scientific evidence proving that genuine formations are created by a process beyond physical manipulation of the crops – and that they are, indeed, created by forces beyond our third-dimensional world.

For example: (1) Timed aerial photographs demonstrate that complex designs covering thousands of square feet have materialised in a matter of minutes. (2) Soil test samples show that the chemical composition of the soil within a glyph is altered. Even in the years *after* a circle is formed, the growth of plants differs in the exact area of the previously laid-down plants, despite the fact that the crops were harvested and the land ploughed and replanted. The new plants are darker in colour and taller than the rest of the field – a genetic

---

* I have already partially described this experience in Chapter 27

memory of the exact configuration, in other words, is still visibly imprinted in the land. (3) Plants within crop circles display anatomical alterations such as abnormally enlarged nodes where the plant stems are bent, pointing to transient high temperatures in the process of laying them down. Indeed, the fact that not a single plant stem is broken is one of the sure-fire signs of a true circle. Rapeseed plants, in particular, are so fragile that it is impossible to bend a stalk without snapping it – and yet in these circles, intricate designs are elegantly forged by a force that leaves not a single stem damaged.

The reason that there is a "season" for circles is that they are formed in crops such as rapeseed, barley, wheat and corn, which in England grow from April to September. I discovered that there are particular fields in which formations appear year after year. The significant factor is usually the proximity of a powerful ancient site such as a stone circle, ceremonial hill or burial mound. The ancestors chose these places for their spiritual earthworks according to the strength of the ley lines present, harnessing the electromagnetic force of Gaia to create powerful temples for ritual and celebration. That same power, amplified by the presence of underlying water, is part of the chemistry inherent in the manifestation of the circles.

I was attracted, like many others, by the sheer beauty, mystery and magic of the formations. I could also sense that the sacred geometry in the patterns called to me on a level that was beyond logic. On viewing an aerial photo of a new glyph, I was sometimes transfixed – compelled to drop everything, reorganise my London schedule and head straight off on the two-and-a-half-hour drive to Avebury. Walking shoes donned, map and coordinates in hand, I was infused with a mounting excitement as I neared each location. Every circle was a brand new adventure.

I became an avid follower of the *Crop Circle Connector* website, run on a volunteer basis by a group dedicated to announcing, investigating and documenting the glyphs. Airplane pilots scan the fields every day to report new circles, followed by ground scouts who take on-site photos and write reports for the website. One of the most interesting aspects of the CCC site is the interpretations of the geometry and messages encoded into the circles, contributed by scientists and metaphysical experts as well as the general public. These range from the portrayal of lunar eclipse sequences, predictions of solar flares and astronomical activities to actual messages from extraterrestrial civilisations to Earth.

One of the game-changers for me was the huge, breath-taking glyph that appeared on the day of the 8.8.8, the 8th of August 2008. I was in Marlborough for the annual Avebury Crop Circle Conference – two solid days of presentations by international scientists, researchers and luminaries offering their insights into the phenomenon. Hearing about the gigantic figure-eight or infinity sign that had appeared that day, I couldn't resist making a detour to check it out before heading back to London. This one was easy to find, located close to a road I knew well.

As I prepared to step into the first circle of the massive pattern, time slowed down and I felt as if I were stepping into a tangible liquid field of plasma. I had an instant and overwhelming urge to spend the night in the field. For some months my guides had been encouraging me to sleep overnight in a circle. They advised me not to be a "crop circle tourist," explaining that it wasn't important how *many* circles I visited, it was about spending more time in those particular ones that were relevant for my personal activation.

Filled with excitement, I sent a message home that something urgent had come up and that I would be back in the morning. I walked back to the car to fetch my sleeping bag and its waterproof "bivvy bag" covering, switched off my phone and settled down for the night in one of the central circles. Around midnight a misty English rain commenced, forcing me to wrap the bivvy bag over my head and huddle in the claustrophobic plastic cocoon on the hard ground. Under normal circumstances this would have made for a horrendous camping experience, but I had entered into a blissful altered state in which I felt the complex fractal geometry of the radiating circles literally being coded into my body, as if I was being rewired.

The rain and clouds lifted just as the dawn broke, allowing me to sit up and meditate in the radiant pink sunrise. The Pleiadian-Sirian

Councils told me that I was ready for a new mission: to lead three *Reconnecting the Codes* workshops in Avebury over the following year. My task was to introduce people to both the crop circles and the power places of Avebury, in order to activate both the people and the land – much in the same way as I was already doing in the *Gaia-and-Tribe* projects.

On the drive back to London I ruminated on where these residential courses could be held, as Avebury is a very small village with no retreat centres. And then I had a brainwave – my favourite B&B in East Kennet had a parking field opposite the house, next to a beautiful little stream. I was sure that if I booked out the whole house for group accommodation, the owners would allow me to erect my belltent in the field to serve as our meeting room. I set the wheels in motion, advertised the courses and the universe worked its magic.

These years fulfilled the predictions of the Star Councils after my activations in South Africa. I was heading *Gaia-and-Tribe Reconnection* projects around the country, branching out beyond Avebury to sites including Wayland Smithy, Uffington White Horse and of course Glastonbury – the heart chakra of our planet.

One of the highlights of the projects was leading a series of group trips to Stonehenge in order to "sing the portal awake," by toning specific mantras in the stone circle. These events were initiated after a visit to the stone circle with Armukara and Urtema during which I was shown the negative astral pollution in the underlying earth. There were remnants of Atlantean sound experiments blocking the portal and therefore preventing the site from transmitting frequencies as it had been designed to. I was guided to book three separate "private entrances" to Stonehenge – hour-long intervals around sunrise where a private group is allowed beyond the tourist barrier and into the actual stone circle. People were thrilled to be able to visit the megalithic monument without a horde of tourists, and the places I offered to the light tribe were fully booked almost overnight.

After the first two entrances, joyful though they were, I wasn't entirely convinced that we were achieving our goal. But midway through the third event we were literally rocked off our feet, the whole group simultaneously experiencing a massive shift of energy as the portal reawakened. We all stopped mid-song, looked at each other in amazement, and proceeded to dance around the stones in a spontaneous celebration.

As we connected the dots on a map to mark the places we had activated in South East England, we were amazed to find perfect geometries emerging – a series of overlapping diamonds. The diamond shape relates to the activation of our crystalline energy body, which coincides with our evolution into multi-dimensional beings. My guides also related the diamonds to the opening of the "Sacred Heart Chakra" in human beings, which marks the transition from self-centred desires, to being able to love all others unconditionally.*

I was asked to put a Sacred Heart Meditation up on my website, where an increasing number of people were accessing these gifts to the tribe. The line was blurring between the paid workshops I was called to facilitate and my service work to Gaia that was offered free of charge – solstice and equinox ceremonies, guided meditations and channelled messages to the tribe of Gaia. I followed the guidance I was given unwaveringly, and there were always enough funds to do what was called for.

All who attended my workshops and ceremonies discovered the power of sound for activating both humans and Gaia. We were called to drum, sing and tone in churches, Neolithic burial chambers, on hilltops, and sometimes locations as unlikely as a parking lot in the centre of a town. My Pleiadian guide Satya urged us thus:

> Oh dear children, turn off your TV's – turn off the noise, turn off the news, tune out the traffic – and sing. Sing as you give healing, sing in the car, sing in the bathtub, sing as you sleep! For your beauteous voices hold healing for all those around. Thus it is

---

* The **Sacred Heart Chakra** (pink in vibration) is slightly higher in the chest than the personal heart chakra (which is emerald green)

that you affect healing within yourselves on a cellular level, as well as within those whom you heal. There is not one of you who cannot issue forth amazing unqualified beauty through your vocal cords.

It is time for you to stop whining about feeling like aliens on the earth plane, about the disconnection between you and your brethren – for you, each one of you, have chosen to be right here, right now at this time in which the ascension plan is indeed taking place. This is not a future event – it is taking place as we speak! You are raising the vibration within your cellular matrix that allows the codes to be unlocked. The 'codes of remembrance' they are often called – which simply means that you re-member who you truly are!

And so it is.

Visiting Stonehenge with my star sisters Urtema & Armukara

Philly & I running towards a
newly discovered circle

Meditating in a crop circle

A moving orb captured on
camera in a crop circle

On Glastonbury Tor

On a Reconnecting the Codes
workshop at Knoll Down

Philly, Armukara, Jana & I at
Wayland Smithy Long Barrow

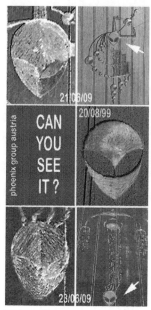

This collage was posted on the CCC site to draw attention to the similarity of the "alien faces" that were incorporated into 3 separate formations over a 10 year period.

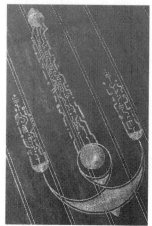

We spent time in 2 mind-blowing crop circles in June 2009, whose "hieroglyphics" portrayed circuit boards, referring to the reconnection of codes within both our physical cells & etheric bodies.

The awesome "6 Julia Set Spiral" incorporated 409 individual circles & spanned 1,500 feet. It represents a complicated mathematical formula that produces beautiful fractal images

The gigantic 8.8.8 crop circle. The tiny dots in the centre are people

CHAPTER 31

Dying in the Garden of the Gods

W hen the Pleiadian-Sirian Councils of Light asked me to put a channelled message on YouTube in 2009, I hadn't even heard of the website! I asked my children about YouTube and they rolled their eyes as teenagers do at the inconceivable ignorance of the adult world, explaining that it was a free site where anyone could post videos. I was puzzled – my guides wanted me to video myself channelling? Never having seen myself in the act, I asked Gabby to film me bringing through a message, just to see what it would look like. Watching it back together we both cringed. As much as I was accustomed to my body jerking and my head nodding as I channelled, I felt too self-conscious to put myself out there that way.

Gabby came up with an alternative option; to upload a message as a sound file, adding some background images to make it into a movie. I was used to recording my meditations, so that felt more doable. At 4 a.m. the following morning I recorded a two-part transmission, the first from the Sirians and the second from the Pleiadians. I set out to make a visual storyline for the recordings on Windows Movie Maker, discovering in the process that the creative aspect of movie-making, although time-consuming, was also tremendous fun! For the first message from the Elakon collective, I included photos and images of Knysna, Stonehenge, sacred geometry, crop circles, star constellations, Jesus and lightships. I uploaded it that evening with the intention of sending a newsletter introducing it the following day. My assumption was that only people who already knew me would watch my offering, as I had no wider audience at that time.

When I checked it the following morning before composing my newsletter, I was dumbfounded to find that I already had hundreds of views! Who were these people and how had they found me? As I watched the viewing number change to thousands in a matter of weeks, my initial resistance to the concept of putting my channelled transmissions "out there" dissipated. I realised what a powerful tool the internet – called the *web of light* by my guides – could be in my service to the light tribe.

Over the following year my students urged me to show myself channelling in my videos because of the energy and mudras that were part of the transmissions, and I eventually succumbed. At the time, most channels were not prepared to show themselves in the act. It was some years later that I saw Darryl Anka transmitting his guide Bashar live on YouTube. When I did, I had an instant jolt of recognition, watching the way his body jerked as his guides connected into his body. I felt immense relief that I was not alone in this strange mission in which I acted as an emissary for more advanced civilisations.

The YouTube experience was, however, sometimes perplexing. A year after my first upload, I received an email telling me that it had been removed because it had been reported for a nudity violation! The offending shot was the painting on the left below, *The Prayer for Peace,* which ran for ten seconds during the message: "The time is imminent in which you transcend the reality that you see around you."

There were indeed naked bodies in the image, but I don't think many people watching it had naughty thoughts while listening to a message about our imminent ascension! I edited and reposted it, substituting the image to the right. Apparently the boy boobs didn't offend anyone.

One of the amazing by-products of my new work was the constant downloading of channelled meditations, which my guides invariably requested I upload onto my website and YouTube channel. These meditations were more often than not affecting actual energy shifts in the people who practised them, as well as teaching spiritual principles. They were often timed to coincide with a solstice or equinox, such as the *Octahedron of Love Meditation*, which was gifted in the lead-up to the June solstice of 2009, designed to protect and uplift us as we moved through a particularly bumpy energetic time window.

Around the same time I channelled the *Unity Consciousness Breath Meditation*, about which my guides said:

> As you consciously breathe prana (intelligent life force) in from above, you awaken your pineal gland. As you breathe prana in from below, you receive healing from our great Mother Earth. As the prana meets in your heart centre, you are tuned into Christ consciousness, the energy of the fifth dimension. These three factors are crucial for your healing, evolution and ascension!

There was a great emphasis on the *prana tube* from 2008 onwards, and many of the meditations that came through the Star Councils included teachings on *activating the prana tube.**

I absolutely loved the way my guides spread these teachings – through providing easy, short, enjoyable meditations for people to use. I followed their guidance to the tee; recording, transcribing and editing the meditations; making some of the sound files into video format for my growing YouTube audience. Many people over those years expressed their gratitude and wonder at how tirelessly I gave myself over in service – but the truth is that this "work" I was being given was an absolute joy! I considered myself blessed beyond my wildest imaginings to be in a position where guidance was constantly available to me, and for my life path to be so obviously playing out in the right direction.

Having been shown the potential of the triple-dates to activate

---

* This **energy tube** or channel runs through all the chakras in the body, up to the top & down to the bottom of your aura. When activated, the **prana tube** extends right up to the heart of the galaxy, the "Great Central Sun" – & right down to the Core Crystal of Gaia – plugging you in above & below; bringing you into a state of "vertical connection" in which it is no longer possible for you to be drawn out of your centre by what is going on around you.

us through my experience in the 8.8.8 crop circle, I published a YouTube in the lead-up to the 9.9.9 calling the light tribe to action. That video was reposted on so many sites that thousands of new people accessed the channelled messages and guided meditations on my website. There was an almost overnight expansion in my world, as my UK workshops suddenly attracted participants from the States, Canada and as far afield as Australia. It was such a joy to meet star brothers and sisters from around the world!

I also started to receive invitations to teach abroad, mostly from the US, where it seemed that channelling was much more widely accepted. As I planned my first teaching venture in the States, my friends joked that Solara An-Ra was "going global!" My first port of call was Boulder, Colorado in January 2010, where I was to teach an Opening to Channel workshop. On the day of my arrival, my host Lisa took me to her friend Cynthia's home, high in the Rockies; an amazing sanctuary in crystalline mountain air. The evening found a small group of us blissfully immersed in an aromatic cedar hot tub on the snowy mountain side, the Pleiades clearly visible above us. As we watched the full moon rising between the mountain peaks, my jetlag evaporated and I was inspired to connect in with my guides. As far as I know there are no rules against channelling naked under the stars in a hot-tub!

The Pleiadian Council gave us information about a medicine wheel that Cynthia would build on her land, giving very specific instructions about the rocks and crystals that were to be used. This was the first of a series of messages concerning a new initiative that called all nations of Gaia to build an interconnecting "web" of medicine wheels. They were to serve the purpose of sacred outdoor temples where groups were called together to celebrate the equinoxes, solstices and triple-dates.

I followed the guidance to put instructions on how to build a medicine wheel and how to lead a ceremony up on my website. My final assignment was to keep an updated list of the wheels that were made, and ceremonies that were to be held around the world in the coming months and years. This focus of leading celebrations on the pivotal dates had been an ongoing theme for me since 2007, but it was now being activated on a much wider scale. Hundreds of people wrote to me about the medicine wheels that they were inspired to build, whether on a mountain top or in their own garden. I also received so many beautiful emails from people who'd made wheels and led ceremonies, sometimes having stepped into a leadership position for the very first time. There was a real sense of light tribe reconnecting with Gaia, remembering how to truly honour Father Sky and Mother Earth, as had our ancestors.

During my first trip to the US it became evident that I was being taken to different locations not only to teach, but also to do Earth-grid reconnection in these places. In Colorado a group of us were asked by the Star Councils to do some healing work in an old Native American site. In Missouri I led a ritual on the snow-topped Cahokia Mounds, and in New York a group of us gathered around a fountain in Central Park for an activation that radiated out through the whole city. Many people who took part in my workshops were also given future missions by the Councils of Light, one example being a healing project on the Mississippi River that had an amazing effect. After the event, the residents of the area reported that there was an actual change in the colour of nearby tributaries of the river – from muddy brown to clear turquoise!

Sometimes individuals who participated in these occasions received a healing or a wake-up call – and in one extraordinary instance, that person was me. The ceremony in question was in the *Garden of the Gods* in Colorado Springs, a beautiful public park where the landscape includes dramatic red rock formations, similar to Sedona. A group of us were guided to perform a ritual in the park to help release some unhappy souls who were trapped in the earth there. They were the spirits of Native American women, still in mourning for their loved ones who'd been killed in a bloody battle many years earlier.

On the chosen day we travelled to the park, located the valley where the battle had occurred, and made a medicine wheel with stones and crystals. After channelling some powerful invocations, we sang and danced around the circle to assist in the release of the trapped souls, all of us moved to tears by the occasion. We gathered afterwards on a big flat rock to relax in the sun and enjoy our well-deserved lunch – at which point, the story acquires a bizarre and disturbing twist.

One of the ladies in our group, Ezeriel, asked me if I could check in with the ancestors to see if they were happy, having been released. I was feeling tired and a bit ungrounded, but I obligingly closed my eyes to see if I could connect with them. Rather than going through my usual pre-channelling routine and asking my guides the question, I tuned straight into the spirits that had been liberated.

Instead of receiving an answer, I felt myself glide towards an elderly woman spirit who was on her journey into the light. Out of curiosity I allowed this to happen, assuming that I was about to receive an answer. I heard her saying her tender farewell to the land and felt myself rising up, my energy joined with hers – oblivious that what was occurring on the outside was extremely alarming. The group told me afterwards that I had stopped talking and had fallen backwards in a strange sort of slow-motion, flat onto the rock face, ostensibly out cold. When I didn't respond to their questions, they checked my pulse and found nothing. I was apparently dead!

Ezeriel, formerly a professional singer, had been told only the day before that she had the power to sing or tone into a person's light bodies in order to heal him or her. She had never used sound for healing, but the situation was desperate and there was no room for hesitation. Her angelic voice rang crystal clear across the plains – and I felt my spirit suddenly slam back into my body on the rock. I was not even aware that I had left my physical body – all of my awareness was in the astral experience into which I'd allowed myself to get sucked.

There are no mistakes, and everything that happened was in perfect timing for the learning of all concerned. For Ezeriel, this incident was directed by her Higher Self. It was her who had asked the question, and it was her who was coerced into stepping up to the challenge – proving to herself in the process that her voice was a potent healing gift.

My personal lesson on this occasion was not to communicate

with disincarnate beings that are not acting in the role of a guide – in this case, a spirit who was in transition between Earth and the other worlds. When you channel it is necessary to be grounded, protected, and in a high vibration. Above all, it is essential that you *always* call in the light and *always* ask for the highest guidance possible, so that the most appropriate guides can answer the questions at hand. I had occasion to remember this several times over the coming years, while working in ancient sites where there are very often curious ancestor spirits present. Discernment is needed in our connection with the other worlds. Intention is everything!

In St. Louis, my next stop, I was greeted by the liveliest bunch of Light Warriors I had yet encountered. I had been slightly concerned about entering the thick of the *Bible Belt,* where my workshop was to be held in a Christian church. My worries proved to be entirely unfounded – the alternative Christian communities in the US were totally open to channelling – very different from the conservative South African churches with which I had grown up. The Missouri group were extremely receptive to my teachings, and the all-day workshop with an audience of 50-plus was very entertaining.

At one point I encouraged them not to put me on a pedestal just because I'm a channel, assuring them that I was a normal person who swears, made mistakes all the time, and so on. A curious woman immediately raised her hand to ask me what swear words I used. I replied that although I never used the f-word to swear against anyone – Egyptian camel owners excluded – my rebellious warrior aspect enjoyed using it as a superlative, as in "Wow, what a fuck-off crystal!" The enthusiasm with which the group embraced the warrior swearing attitude was hysterical – they waved me off the following day, shouting after the taxi, "You're a fuck-off teacher Solara!" and "Have a fuck-off flight home Solara!"

I laughed all the way to the airport. Never take your spiritual path too seriously – if there is no laughter, something is amiss.

Rocky Mountain High, with my host Cynthia

In the mountain snow

In a Colorado Crystal Bowl Temple

With Gabriella in New York

CHAPTER 32
Flying the Nest

B ack from my first US teaching tour, I looked at my agenda for
2010 in absolute wonder. In addition to my assignments all over
the UK, my program included Amsterdam, Peru, Mexico, and several
destinations in the States, including Los Angeles, New York, Sedona
and Mount Shasta. The Pleiadians had prophesied that my life would
change completely after taking on my Higher Self name, and I was
witnessing that transformation. As Solara An-Ra, I had stepped fully
into the role of a Warrior of the Light, Earth-keeper and teacher.

There was one aspect of the missions I'd been given that
pushed me out of my comfort zone. I was being asked to lead trips in
countries that I had never previously visited – the first being to Machu
Picchu in Peru for the March equinox. The programs I'd offered in
England had always been preceded by my own personal explorations
and assimilation of the energies at each site. But my guides assured
me that it wasn't necessary to have previous knowledge of a place to
be a true guide – I simply had to tune into the energies in each place
we visited, ask for guidance, and the magic would unfold.

The first step in the manifestation of my Peruvian journey was
to hire a travel company to organise the accommodation and internal
travel. Through a series of synchronicities I came across a small
shamanic retreat company based in Cusco. What I was requesting was
not their usual gig, but I instantly made a good connection with the
coordinator, Angel, who devised an itinerary that allowed me to offer
the expedition at an affordable price. My mission in Peru was initiated
– *Spring Equinox in Machu Picchu* was up on my website!

A few weeks after advertising the journey, I realised that it
would in fact be autumn in March in the southern hemisphere, and
not spring. Blushing with embarrassment at my slip-up, I changed
the title to the more neutral *March Equinox in Machu Picchu*. Bookings
came in steadily, much to my delight, and preparations went ahead

smoothly ... until a shocking email pinged its way into my inbox only nine days before the departure date. Angel informed me, with great regret, that due to mudslides washing away the rail track, we wouldn't be able to visit Machu Picchu! Cusco and the sacred valley were still on the program, but the proposed change of itinerary would include Lake Titicaca instead.

"He-e-e-e-lp!" I screamed inwardly. How could this be happening? My guides were as cool as you like, assuring me that we were truly destined to visit Lake Titicaca, and that the new schedule would allow us to visit some other sites that were more powerful even than the much revered Machu Picchu. When I questioned why they had asked me to go to Machu Picchu if it wasn't to be, they replied that it had been necessary to attract certain people who would not otherwise have booked on – but who were absolutely meant to be there!

Blushing even deeper, I amended the title for the third and last time to *March Equinox at Lake Titicaca*. I wrote to the group, offering to refund anyone who no longer wished to take part. I included a message from the Star Councils assuring them that there are no mistakes, ever, and that the voyage would be exactly what we had all called for on a Higher Self level. To my great relief, not one of the sixteen participants pulled out.

On arriving in Cusco my heart melted open in recognition. I had seen these green mountains and breathed this crystalline air in another lifetime. The group bonded almost instantly and we felt like children, open-mouthed in awe at the delights we discovered around every corner. We chewed cocoa leaves to help combat the crazy altitude, meditated on mountain tops, trekked through Inca villages, played with local children and channelled under the stars. A tale was woven that united past lives with present, confirming the role we were playing in fulfilling our contracts with each other and with Pachamama.

The channelled messages we received in Peru came not only from the Star Councils of Light, but also from a host of Earth guardians and enlightened masters. In Sacsayhuaman, the first temple complex we visited, the Pleiadian Councils decoded some of the teachings of the "Jesus Christ Light Child." As we stood in circle on a mountain peak, a great white statue of Jesus visible on an adjacent peak, we heard these words in a new light. "As you give, so you receive. As you give, so you receive." On the third utterance, they added one word: "As you give, so you receive, *multiplied*." This biblical phrase has echoed within me ever since; an internal mantra reinforcing the universal law of attraction and the power of giving selflessly from the infinite generosity of the awakened heart.

We moved from Cusco to the fascinating mountain ruins of Ollantaytambo, and on to a charming retreat in Urubamba in the sacred valley. In the terraced amphitheatre of Moray in Maras, I saw in my inner vision the remains of an underground *City of Light*. For the first time, an individual Arcturian being spoke directly through me, teaching on the purpose and history of the crystalline pyramid, now unused, directly below us.

The voice that came through me was comically squeaky and a bit robotic, reducing us all to giggles. This was a precursor to a remarkable occurrence with a group on Silbury hill later that year, in which a female Arcturian, with my permission, entered my body in order to demonstrate how they are able to direct energy at will. In the dark of a moonless English night, this sweet star being had raised my arms and pointed in a forward direction with my fingers. Astonishingly, we had all witnessed light shooting out of my fingertips like lasers!

Our Peruvian guide, Angel – angel by name and by nature – constantly looked out for us. He placated authorities who were suspicious of our spiritual activities, and assisted us in accessing parts of temples that were usually closed to tourists. He also arranged for eight of my group to partake in an ayahuasca ceremony on our fourth night – an event not originally on our agenda. Some of their experiences, narrated around the fire the following evening, were profoundly moving – far deeper than my own ayahuasca trips in the Amazon. When the student is ready, the teacher will appear.

A highlight of Peru for me was an impromptu trip to Amaru

Meru, the multi-dimensional *Star Gate of the Gods*. As I placed my head to the "door" of the great stone edifice, my third eye opened and I was catapulted into the stars. It was a remarkable feeling, similar to that in the sarcophagus of the Great Pyramid – a spontaneous shift out of 3-D. Discussing our unique experiences at the star gate, everyone in group agreed that it had been an essential part of our quest in Peru – one that we would not have shared had we stuck to our original itinerary.

In every way the journey felt perfectly synchronised. The long hours on the bus down to Lake Titicaca had been the one part of the new agenda that had caused me some concern – but it turned out to be the perfect way to see the country's interior, breath-taking views thrilling us around every bend. On our first evening at the great lake, we were honoured to receive a message directly from the *Manu* or Great Spirit of Titicaca. In the deep booming voice of a wise elder she gave us permission to travel on her waters, requesting also that we assist in reconnecting the light grid between her and Machu Picchu. This we did through working with crystals and gifting them to the waters in several rituals on the lake. We spent our final night at the lake on the island of Amantani, celebrating the equinox with a moving ceremony around a fire under a canopy of brilliant stars.

Back in London after our incredible adventure in Peru, I found it hard to settle back into my domestic environment. I looked at my program for the remainder of the year, reflecting on how much time I would be away from London, and a radical plan started hatching.

I was feeling increasingly frustrated living in a big house and garden that constantly demanded time, effort and money to upkeep. The life I had built with Jeremy had centred around our beloved home, but the dinner parties, barbeques and family gatherings of the past were no longer part of my movie. The children were super independent, Max in university digs in Brighton and Gabby nearing the end of college. Jeremy had recently remarried to a Brazilian woman with a young son. Subject to how he and the children felt, my proposal was to give him his old home back in a few months' time – cats, dogs and all. I was ready to throw everything safe, domestic and suburban to the winds!

My friends, family and clients were all shocked when I announced my plan. They found it impossible to believe that I, having always been very home-orientated, would be happy to simply rent a room in London between my travels. Jeremy was nevertheless thrilled at the prospect of moving back into the house; living with Gabby full-time and Max in his uni holidays. "But what about all your things?" he asked me, raising his eyebrows when I replied, "I don't care about things – I don't need a home anymore!"

My main concern was for Gabby, then in her final year of college. I was worried that she would feel like I was deserting her, even if London was still to be my home base. Jeremy and I agreed that it was the right thing for her to be with him again, she needed a full-time parent – but how would she react to the idea of living with his new family? I never imagined that her concerns over my imminent departure would be focused in an entirely different direction.

Gabby understood my path more than most, having been surrounded by my spiritual activities, stories, books and clients her whole life. Over the years, I had told her what my guides had prophesied for her future, but as she hadn't seemed overly interested, I'd assumed it was a case of "in one ear, out the other." Thus, when I approached her nervously with my proposal to move out, I was amazed at her immediate and urgent response: "Don't tell me this means that I'm not going to become the 'Light Child' your guides said I would be? How am I going to do that without you?"

I burst out laughing in relief, reassuring her that I would be there for her every step of the way. I had no idea that she took her spiritual path so seriously – she had apparently just been waiting till the elusive "later" when she wasn't so busy being a teenager! Once she knew that she had a limited time living with me, Gabriella Light Child sprang into action.

She enrolled on my next four-week meditation course, enlisting the participation of several of her friends along the way. I offered some teenager-only sessions where she and her friends had their first experiences of feeling the energy of crystals, learning how to see one another's auras, and practising chakra meditation and breathing techniques.

In one of these classes I guided the group through a grounding process that concluded with them feeling the love of Gaia pouring back up through their bodies. As Gabby visualised this, she was suddenly filled with a bright blue-white light, as a star being merged with her body. She physically felt her head taller and fingers longer than usual and light pouring out of her skin, much like my encounter with the Arcturian on Silbury Hill. She was bubbling with excitement as she recounted what had happened on the way home, grinning from ear to ear. The Pleiadians were making themselves known to her in their own unique way – so heart-warmingly sweet and friendly, it made her cry.

Shortly after this she took part in my *Opening to Channel* workshop, which helped her to understand the purpose of guides and the importance of the path that I had chosen. She had previously only witnessed *my* channelling – seeing other participants connecting with their Higher Selves and guides was fascinating for her. It was a wonderful bonding experience for the two of us, and such an unexpected blessing at a juncture where I had been anxious about losing her. The universe was demonstrating very clearly that when you are brave enough to follow your dreams, unexpected gifts are inevitably showered upon you.

Along with my home, it was time to give up my therapist identity. I'd spent years building up a thriving healing and therapy practice in London, but my passion had gradually shifted away from one-on-one healing. This was yet another decision that surprised and puzzled everyone, not least of all my faithful clients. It just wasn't done to give up a successful practice and branch out on an unconventional tangent. But wasn't that exactly what I'd succeeded in twenty years before, when – against the advice of everyone around me – I'd left my teaching job to become a therapist? I was going with the flow, and my river was flowing inexorably towards my global soul family!

I decided to coordinate leaving Portal Close and the clinic with my "Mayan Elder" transition – my 52nd birthday. I had first looked into Mayan astrology after the Sirians mentioned the Tzolkin in my first YouTube message. Never having related to Western astrology, my studies of the Tzolkin were a revelation. In this system your *galactic signature*, based on your birthdate, describes not only your personality traits, but also your purpose in this particular incarnation. I learnt that my signature, *Blue Electric Hand,* denotes a person who is a natural manifestor, and who is designed to be a portal or channel between dimensions, having the gift of oracular divination. This description was so astoundingly accurate that I delved deeper, discovering that one's 52nd birthday is considered the exact point at which you enter a second cycle, transitioning into your *wisdom years.*

I was just about to cross this threshold – what better time to make the shift into my new life? I organised a final ceremony to take place in my healing room on my birthday; a send-off into my wisdom years. My inner circle gathered for this precious occasion – a council of London goddesses who had been at the core of the Gaia-and-Tribe projects, including Philly, Urtema and Armukara.

I was in awe of the new horizons which had opened for me through the dissolution of my marriage. It had never occurred to me that being with Jeremy – always encouraging and supportive – could be holding me back on my path. We can never know the gifts that will manifest from a give-away – until we actually let go.

Our welcome ceremony with the shamans in Peru

Our awesome Peru Light Tribe

Around a fire in the Sacred Valley

Angel and the shamans

Smudging the tribe at Sacsayhuaman

The women of the Floating Islands

Mayan Elder Gathering ~ entry into my wisdom years
Left to right: Tatanka, Pascale, Philly, Armukara, me, Jana, Urtema

With a warrior guide in Tulum

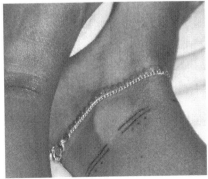

My first stop as a nomad:
the Yucatan, Mexico

A jungle initiation: my '13 Mayan tones'
ankle tattoo

CHAPTER 33

Telos & the 10.10.10

Icelebrated my new *Nomad Light Warrior* status with a month in the Yucatan peninsula of Mexico, where Ezeriel had generously offered me her apartment in exchange for some workshops. My intention was to focus on a book I was writing, which necessitated some time-out from the world – but that was a seriously flawed plan. How had I imagined I would get any writing done in a setting of exotic jungles, gorgeous beaches and Mayan temples? Even more than the ocean, I was magnetised to the Yucatan cenotes – crystal clear lakes sunk into stunning underground limestone caves. I have always found lakes to be the most magical places to swim; immersing oneself in their still, cool depths is like entering the planetary body and listening to the heartbeat of Gaia. It was truly thrilling to dive into deep blue-green cenotes surrounded by primeval water ferns and turquoise crabs.

As I visited the temples of Chichen Itza, Tulum, Coba and Ek Balam, my guides spoke frequently of the importance of the triple-dates in the lead up to the 2012 solstice. They said:

> We see in your future time-line that there are more gathered together on the 10.10.10 than have ever been gathered as light tribe on your planet. And we ask you all to be holding clear or rose quartz crystals as you connect with each other, with the crystal skulls, with the crystal beds of Gaia, and with the core crystal herself. We celebrate this day and occasion with you – the 10.10.10 – and the greater occasion of your awakening as light beings on Gaia now.

There was indeed an escalating sense of both urgency and excitement as 2012 loomed closer. People were waking up to the fact that something special was happening on Earth, and the spiritual lethargy that had blanketed our planet during the Piscean age was evaporating. I experienced this directly through the ever-expanding list of ceremonies on my website and the increasing interest in my courses and sacred site journeys. As the 10.10.10 approached I was overwhelmed with applicants for my Sedona and Mount Shasta workshops – so much so that I was pressurised into expanding the participant total for Sedona to 22, and the Mount Shasta group to 33!

Having dealt with the complicated logistics of leading 16 in Peru, I had no idea how I would manage the accommodation, meals and transport for such big groups. I was reminded to simply ask for help and trust in the universe – et voila! Two enthusiastic students stepped forward to act as assistants, while others volunteered to act as drivers. After a bit of research I found perfect venues for both workshops – a hotel right in the centre of the Sedona vortices and a lovely resort near Mount Shasta, with wooden cabins in a fragrant pine forest. When we choose to be of service, every single thing we need to achieve our highest purpose is provided.

Sedona was a pilgrimage place for our ancestors, much like Uluru in Australia – it was never meant to be inhabited and developed. At our first meeting on Cathedral Rock we were told that the settlements in the area were disrupting the natural flow between the energy vortices – and that our mission was to assist in reconnecting them. This we joyfully did, meditating and toning at all the main vortices, finally grounding our work deep into the core crystal in the hollow Schnebly Bowl. Our last day included a wonderful sound activation at Red Rock Crossing, after which we swam and frolicked in the water to celebrate the completion of our work.

We immediately hit the road again to join the larger group who were gathering at Stewart Mineral Springs, a rustic but beautiful resort on the banks of a creek in the Mount Shasta foothills. The Star Councils requested that our first step should be to visit Pluto Caves, in the outlying area, in order to ask the ancestors for permission to enter the portal of the mountain. This is a key to accessing the true power of any sacred place – to enter with respect and humility, and only after receiving permission from the guardians of the land.

Pluto's Cave is a partially collapsed lava tube from an ancient eruption of Mount Shasta – the perfect place for us to connect with both the mountain and the inner earth. The photos we took inside the cave showed that the spirits of the land and the ancestors were all around us – there are so many orbs that it's difficult to see the group!

Before embarking on the Mount Shasta tour, I had heard stories of Telos, the Lemurian city directly beneath the mountain. My only experience of underground civilisations was my brief encounter with the remains of the crystal pyramid in the Peruvian amphitheatre of Moray. I was curious to see if I would have an encounter with the Telos community – and I was not disappointed.

On our first day on the slopes of Shasta, our guide led us in a meditation designed to take us into the underground city. Halfway through the meditation I was suddenly filled with light as Adama – the High Priest of Telos about whom I had read – literally came into my body. His white robes energetically adorned me, the sleeves falling from my upraised arms, his long soft pale hair caressing my shoulders.

I waited impatiently until the guided meditation was complete, almost exploding afterwards into a transmission that began: "I am Adama!" In his deep, wise voice he introduced us to the ways of his subterranean culture and the warmth of his welcome was so touching, it was hard not to cry. As I perceived this civilisation, its people encompassed the high vibration of the star beings, but were more like humans, having lived inside our physical planet for so many thousands of years.

Stewart Mineral Springs was an absolute treat after the dusty mountains of Sedona – we spent our free time soaking in Victorian bathtubs filled with healing mineral water and chilling out in the enormous wood-burning sauna. From the heat of the sauna we raced outside and plunged naked into the icy creek waters, squealing like children. Receiving a massage at the resort was also a fantastic, if surreal, experience – my handsome young Native American Indian therapist relayed psychic messages about my past and future as he worked on me.

The culmination of this journey was the public ceremony on the slopes of Mount Shasta on the 10.10.10. When we arrived at the mountain clearing we had chosen for the ritual, we were delighted to find that a group of Indigo kids had already made a heart-shaped altar and fireplace especially for us. These young people had the vibe of the sixties love children; camping rough on the snow-clad mountain, playing guitars and drums, living outside of mainstream society. We had encountered them on the previous day, inviting them to share our meditation and picnic lunch, and they had reciprocated in this beautiful way for our ceremony.

We were concerned that people would struggle to find our location, seemingly in the middle of nowhere, but at the appointed hour 144 people magically materialised for this truly wonderful gathering. As we formed a huge circle under an impeccable blue sky, the atmosphere was charged with excited anticipation. The message I channelled from an elder of the White Feather tribe was met with great "AHOs" from the crowd. The enthusiasm in the circle was so contagious, we beamed like Cheshire cats, high on the crisp mountain air and the united energy of love love love.

Our mission on the 10.10.10 was to assist in raising the planet into crystalline frequency. After activating our prana tubes through the *Unity Consciousness Breath* meditation, we were directed to hold our charged crystals and tone specific sounds: "OM" as we sent our love into the crystal beds and core crystal – "AH" as we received her love into our hearts – "EEH" as we sent this energy into the crystalline grid of Gaia 60 miles above our planet. Our final chant was the word "PEACE," sending love and peace to all sentient beings on Gaia, our angelic voices echoing across the valley. As we stood silently holding hands after this amazing activation, there was a visible radiant glow emanating from our circle. We were told that on this day humankind was making a great leap into the fifth-dimensional ascension frequencies and we could *feel* it, right through to our bones.

2010 Sedona light tribe

Teaching in Sedona

In the beautiful red rock vortices of Sedona

Ancestor spirit orbs in Pluto's Cave

10.10.10 ceremony on Mount Shasta

CHAPTER 34
Breaking the Annunaki Cord

At the close of my first sojourn in Egypt my guides had foretold that I would return to the land of Khem as the leader of a large and joyful party, and that I would be greatly supported on the second venture by the group. My decision to fulfil this prediction was made spontaneously in Peru, when a student asked me when I was due to revisit Egypt. I explained how vulnerable I had felt there previously and said that I would only feel comfortable returning with "a man at my back." At this point a gentleman in the group stepped forward, committing to support me on any future trip that I might undertake. Chris was a lovely man who, without being asked, was already unofficially assisting me in Peru. I had imagined that "the man" would be a partner, but in the moment that Chris made the offer, a deep wave of knowing washed over me: *The time is now!*

I committed to leading a group through the temples of the Nile in January 2011, aware that this expedition was being co-created on a Higher Self level by all those who were to share it with me. The momentum that had resulted in my attracting 33 attendees in Mount Shasta was still rolling, and I agreed to take the same size group to Egypt, many participants from my 2010 workshops joining me once again. There was a palpable acceleration in the air - I felt the driving force of the universe behind my sails, propelling the boat of my destiny forward at full speed.

From the very first gathering of the group on the Giza plateau, the feeling of *soul family* in the group was undeniable. It evoked a wonderful sense that we, as *Family of Light*, were there to support each other on our journey. Those who were already friends embraced those who were new to the group wholeheartedly. One dear lady who had come with a friend, never having previously participated in any spiritual activity, was blown away by the love and acceptance of the group. Five years later she shared in an email: "I will never ever forget my trip with you to Egypt. I always tell my friends and family that you were the nicest group of people that I have ever come across."

On the first night the Star Councils said that every one of us had lived in ancient Egypt in a previous lifetime. We were informed that we had been called back to fulfil or nullify certain contracts, as was appropriate for our ascension process. Karma was apparently no longer playing out in the old-school way. In some cases, it was possible to over-ride karmic contracts in order to walk the highest path of service in this lifetime. They said that many of us were as yet unaware of the intentions of our Higher Selves in this visit to Egypt, but that all would unfold effortlessly as we travelled from one temple to the next. The messages we received that night were so profound that it was almost overwhelming to some participants. There was a feeling of something momentous unfolding, which overrode the usual "getting to know each other" introductions.

Moreover, the Star Councils said that we were all to go through a series of initiations, just as the spiritual leaders of ancient Egypt had done as they progressed through the schools of Horus. We were immediately catapulted into the first ceremony, right there in the garden of our hotel under the star-studded desert sky. This was an initiation into the Order of Melchizedek – an occasion for which we had apparently been preparing through a series of tests. Under the guidance of the Pleiadian Council we arranged ourselves in pairs, facing one another. We were instructed to place a drop of Egyptian amber on our partner's third eye while sounding a tone, followed by the invocation: "You have been deemed worthy, Child of Light, to carry the light of the Order of Melchizedek; that you may be in service for the Divine Plan of Ascension on Gaia." It felt like we were "knighting" each other; conferring a great and solemn honour, and simultaneously remembering how we had performed similar rites in our roles as priests and priestesses in other lifetimes.

There were many times during our passage through the temples in which we experienced the same feeling that we were re-enacting a ritual from another age. The most powerful instance for me was in the King's Chamber of the Great Pyramid of Giza. This time I had organised a two-hour private entrance, which was an absolute delight after the stress of my last visit. The whole group had tuned into the King's Chamber the night before, asking for the presence of four archangels, one in each corner of the space, to prepare the chamber for our imminent entry. As we entered the chamber the following morning before sunrise, dressed in ceremonial white, we felt their presence holding a high vibration intact.

Each person seemed to know what to do without instruction. Some set up an altar in the centre of the room, some stepped forward as assistants to help people in and out of the sarcophagus, and others still reconnected the sacred geometry of the pyramid through light language and sound. It was impossible to imagine that we had only joined as a group two days before - we were so in tune with each other. The entire interlude was like being in a movie; in an altered reality or lucid dream. We were reactivating memories of the ancient mystery schools in the collective consciousness, for the benefit of our children and future generations.

As we journeyed on down the Nile, the experiences we had in the temples were completely unique for each person, according to their present and past life contracts. In one temple someone would be ecstatic at being reunited with the Isis or Hathor frequency, while another would be beset by the painful memory of a betrayal. Past life memories of old loves, positions of power and responsibility, bloody battles and oppression from corrupted leaders – all these and more resulted in an abundance of laughter and tears, and the releasing and healing of old wounds.

Above and beyond these personal healings and activations, was our joint mission to reconnect the original light frequencies in the temples. On the bus, boat or train, on the way to our next destination, I would channel for the group and we would learn our specific task in that place: to assist the ancestors in healing something from the past; to reconnect the light grid; or to repair the connection between that temple and another. In Edfu, for example, we freed energies that allowed it to function as a portal once more, reconnecting it with Dendera. Ley lines within the Nile waters were activated between the two temples, reinstating the union of the divine masculine and feminine.

Egypt was in a very delicate political position at that time – a revolution was brewing and the military were given orders to restrict any suspicious group activities. Translated, that amounted to police officials following and hassling us, shouting, "No pray! No meditation!" at the slightest hint of our congregating anywhere in a temple. We became experts at avoiding the officials, distracting them in one area so that others could get on with whatever our work was. Rather than letting the military interference aggravate us, it became part of the adventure.

In the temple of Seti we were guided to sing out our Higher Self names throughout the temple, in order to announce our presence and simultaneously receive downloads. Without planning our tactics, we instinctively dispersed into every nook and cranny of the building and started toning, thoroughly confusing the guards who were surrounded by echoing angelic voices from all sides. In instances such as these we operated as one unit, everybody intuitively executing their part of the mission, as perfectly tuned instruments working for the Divine Plan of Gaia.

I developed a comical way of channelling in public, standing with my group in front of a new temple, pretending to be a conventional guide giving an explanation about the site. I would wave my hands in this direction and that, like an air hostess showing the exit-doors, while bringing through a message about our purpose there. In many instances, the information the Star Councils offered concerning the temple at hand contradicted the conventional history given in the guide books.

We escaped the outbreak of violence in Egypt by a hair's breadth, departing only days before the revolution started. We were told, in fact, that our work had assisted greatly in preparing the people to stand up to their oppressors. Through healing the past, we had helped to manifest the beginnings of a new future for the people of Egypt.

Despite the military presence, there were still guards willing to reveal some of the secrets of their temples – the secret agents of light with whom I was familiar from my previous trip. One such of these played a vital role in my karmic healing in the last temple we visited.

In the process of our work there, I had started feeling an oppressive heaviness weighing down on me, and had consequently separated myself from the group. Looking around for somewhere to meditate undisturbed, I came across a location where an underground passage was roped off. I stood staring at it, rooted to the spot, when out of nowhere a guard appeared. Without consultation he unhooked the rope, signalled me to go down the small stone staircase and immediately attached the rope behind me so that my privacy was assured.

Goosebumps covering my body, I descended the narrow passage, using my phone as a torch to study the hieroglyphs adorning the walls. As I reached the end of the corridor, the light illuminated a single image of a humanoid lizard being. The carving was unlike any I had seen in the many temples we had visited – I knew instinctively that it was an Annunaki, and that this was the contract that I had come to sever in the land of Khem.

Three years earlier I had accessed a memory of a previous lifetime in which I was one of the female humans prostituted to the lizard beings, during the epoch in which they held God-like roles on our planet. I had buried this memory, ashamed to acknowledge any connection with them. As I stared at this carving, the memories and feelings associated with this past life emerged. My guides stepped in to help me sever the energetic cord to the past with a powerful cord-cutting process, releasing me from its oppressive grip. As I forgave myself and the beings who had sought to control me, a rush of energy flooded back into my body. The feeling of a heavy responsibility binding me to Egypt was lifted from my shoulders.

My inclination has always been to focus attention away from our history with these dark ones, who have sought to manipulate our minds and our perception of reality. But I am not without compassion for the lizard race, who do not have the ability to feel emotions the way we do, and who therefore plot for their survival through an agenda of control.

All that is needed to be free of their hold over us is to truly own our own power and sovereignty. The past is the past. It has no power over us, other than we allow through our thought and beliefs. Forgiveness and compassion for all of our past roles are needed.

The support from the group that I received in this second journey was deeply touching. Aside from Chris and Armukara, there were other angels who stepped in whenever help was needed, my beautiful sis-stars DebRa, Janna and KeenaRa in particular. As much as I led the way and assisted the group, their assistance through my own passage of rites was indispensable – the end result of which was the release from karmic cords that had bound me for many lifetimes.

Although I never voiced this in so many words, they understood, as expressed by one of the group afterwards in this touching personal message: "I really felt deeply that we 33 had come there to help you Solara, to access the next level. I didn't need to know how and why. We all came for Gaia, for Egypt and of course for ourselves – but in a higher way for you. And that was beautiful for all of us."

Teaching on the bus

I finally got on that camel!

One of the Temple guards who assisted me in the King's Chamber of the Great Pyramid

Our ceremony inside the Kings Chamber of the Great Pyramid of Giza

Early morning Sphinx

Our amazing Egypt light tribe outside the Temple of Isis

Ezeriel initiating me in the Isis Temple

PART 7

The Time Is Now!

CHAPTER 35
The Crying Game

The crying began in June 2011 on my second group trip to Peru. I had flown into Cusco three days early in order to adjust to the altitude and settle in. My guides had been telling me for months that I needed recharging, and had advised me to use the free time before the group arrived to relax. I was so caught up in action mode, however, that I convinced myself that a channelled solstice message needed to be sent out urgently. I spent every spare minute editing the film and then running around town, fruitlessly trying to find an internet connection strong enough to upload the video.

On the morning of the third day I finally let go of the unsuccessful project, smudged myself, did my daily practises and connected in. Instead of receiving the expected guidance about Peru, the first message I received was, "If you continue to ignore our guidance and push yourself, dear one, you will not survive." As the word "survive" escaped my lips, I burst out crying.

The glaring truth was staring me in the face – I was totally exhausted. The amount of travelling I had done over the past two years was taking its toll. I'd been zooming back and forth across time zones, packing and unpacking, yo-yo'ing from summer to winter, dry climate to moist, and dealing with the inevitable jetlag. I also had to recognise that having no home base and fluctuating between friends' houses and hotels no longer felt liberating. I knew I was ungrounded because I was forgetful and was losing things – earlier in the year I had left my only suitcase on the plane to Mexico, never to be recovered.

As I sat there reflecting, an avalanche of tears began flowing from my heart, like a wellspring that had been trapped underground for centuries. Try as I might, I could not stop crying. I hid in my room the whole day, ordering lunch in, and pulling myself together that evening at the very last minute for our first group meeting. I was open with the group about my emotional state, and was touched by their support and understanding.

Over the weeks that followed, whenever I failed to notice the signs that I needed to slow down or ask for help, I would receive a sharp wake-up call. One of these occasions was at Sacsayhuaman where our tour guide showed us a smooth channel in the solid rock face, apparently used by children as a slide on the weekends. Fearless, or perhaps foolish as ever, I took up the challenge. Only when I was hurtling down the fifty-foot rock did I realise that landing at that speed on hard ground was likely to result in a severe whiplash! My attempt to land on bent legs to absorb the impact resulted in a painful fracture of my sacrum, as I fell sideways onto my butt. Talk about a root chakra alert – it was almost comical that I couldn't sit on my bum for weeks without being reminded that something was painfully wrong! Root chakra issues are about home, safety and security. It was patently obvious that I had been without the security of a proper home for too long.

On this second trip to Peru, the long-awaited visit to Machu Picchu finally materialised. It was all the more precious for the wait! In the mysterious morning mist, I channelled an ancestor shaman of the site, who explained why permission had been given to build a city in this holy place. He said that the ancient guardians of the land had foreseen that after the demise of the Incan civilisation, western people would be attracted to visit the ruins. This would come to pass at a time when the people of Gaia urgently needed to remember their connection with the earth.

Dear reader, we are these people! Without the ruined city, we would most likely never be motivated to travel to those holy mountains – and as the shaman explained to us, it was the *mountains* surrounding the site, rather than the ruins themselves, that held the potential to both ground us into the core crystal of Mother Earth and reconnect our codes. This was exactly what several of us had already intuited during our exploration of the site. I discovered that the spectacular peak of Putucusi, in particular, continuously emitted an energy that we could receive *when* we were grounded and our hearts were open.

As our group made the transition between Peru and Bolivia I

asked my guides and the angels for assistance, as I was still crying at the drop of a hat. My prayers were answered immediately in the form of DebRa and Keenara, participants respectively from New Jersey and Vancouver, who were Earth Angels in every way. Unasked, they stepped into assistant roles, holding the focus of the group while we were moving between sites, and taking the pressure off me. They had attended several of my workshops, and were thus in tune with both my work and their own guidance.

Throughout our journey I channelled a series of "Energy Lessons," which made us feel as though we were travelling in a cosmic classroom. My guides said:

> Babaji, the Christ-child of India, works with us through Solara An-Ra to awaken you to your powers now. You will learn, like the yogic masters of old, to hold sufficient prana in your bodies that you are able to transcend the need to breathe through the physical lungs. You will learn to use your breath to move into transcendent states of bliss. You will learn to control your energy and light bodies; to contract and expand your light as the situation demands. And thus will you step outside of the sphere of influence of the manipulators entirely – you will be the fearless Warriors of the Light that are the new leaders of Gaia.

It finally dawned on me that Babaji's presence had *always* been over-lighting me, and that this was the reason so many of my channelled messages were focussed on prana and the power of the conscious breath. It was such a joyful revelation to feel His sweet presence with us through the lessons – and so amazing to do pranayama in the intoxicating mountain air of the Andes.

A theme of crystal healing and activation was initiated as we charged crystals on the Island of the Sun, activated Lake Titicaca through the gifting of crystals, and created a sacred stone altar in the mountains above Sorata. Our venture was in so many ways healing and inspiring, but for many of us, it also proved to be challenging.

Some of our group were detained at the Peru-Bolivia border because of a political strike, making their mission to meet us in Sorata difficult and frightening. Others experienced difficulty walking at high altitudes, or were laid ill as clearing of their bodies took place. My vulnerability, as I continued to cry on and off right through the journey prompted others in the group to express and explore their own wounds. We were being challenged to move through our fears and past the obstacles that were placed in our way.

Back in London after the trip, still severely shaken by the emotional melt-down, I took a good hard look at my life. Friends were urging me to slow down, and to reduce my workload by employing an assistant. It was difficult for me to delegate when I was so used to running the show, but I fought through my resistance and employed Tatanka Nehweh, a lovely Zimbabwean woman who had studied meditation and channelling with me.

It wasn't an option to cancel what remained of my 2011 program – my three September workshops in Canada and the *11.11.11 Sedona Conference* were already nearly fully booked. The only immediate solution was to make time for a proper holiday. I decided to revisit Hawaii for a whole month, in an attempt to recharge and re-set. I had always wanted to return to the islands since the "floating coconut" incident in my youth, and it worked perfectly as a stopover on the way to Canada. I read about the fire goddess Pele, who welcomed some and spat others off the islands, and wondered if I would pass muster the second time around.

Within a few days of landing on the island of Maui, I had organised a room in a house in Makawao, a beautiful upcountry town near Paia. I decided to stay in a communal house so as not to be on my own, and did everything within my power to relax, make friends, explore and nurture myself. Massages, swimming in the ocean and walking on the beach were all delightful, but I was still very tearful and was periodically experiencing a crushing loneliness. The feeling of something missing reinitiated my default drive to action. I am a natural manifestor; a characteristic *blue hand* galactic signature in Mayan astrology. I hatched a misguided plan for a Maui workshop in 2012, and busied myself visiting retreat venues and researching sacred sites on the island.

Unsurprisingly, my busy-ness didn't make me feel any better, and two weeks into my visit, I sunk into a black night of the soul. I kept thinking, "I'm in Hawaii, everyone's dream holiday destination, and I'm not having fun – something is seriously wrong!" My guides had told me many times that I must enter my next relationship consciously, rather than my usual "rush in, work out the details later" approach. I knew, in other words, that I was preparing myself for a soul mate, and was to resist any casual affairs. But on this particular morning, I cried out to the universe to grant me a divine dispensation in the form of a holiday romance – one that wouldn't jeopardise my future soul partnership. I really couldn't think of anything else that was guaranteed to switch off my compulsion to work, and get me to relax! My appeal was miraculously and almost instantaneously answered when I drove over to the wild side of the island in order to explore the *Seven Pools of Oheo*.

I decided to sleep on the beach after spending time at the pools, reluctant to embark on the tiresome drive home on rough roads in the darkening twilight. The following morning, tired and grumpy after a rough night with the mosquitos, I stopped at an outdoor café just after dawn for a much needed cup of Earl Grey. Sitting opposite me was the only other early-bird, a weathered cowboy with long silver-blonde hair.

After introducing ourselves we were silent. I was feeling tearful and not up to small talk, and he seemed comfortable just sitting in the morning sun, listening to the sound of the birds. After about ten minutes I looked over at him through my sunglasses, observing him happily puffing on his roll-up, demanding nothing from me. It occurred to me that if I shared something of my pain with this stranger, it might lessen the burden. Michael was older than me and I wasn't attracted to him, but I instinctively trusted and liked him.

"I'm feeling like shit this morning," I started up wryly. "What's up?" he asked with a kind smile, offering me a napkin to dry a tear that had escaped and was trickling down my cheek. Hesitantly I started talking while Michael listened intently, holding a safe space for my outpouring. He was a natural listener who thought carefully before giving any feedback, but the few words he spoke touched a cord and shifted me out of my slump. It turned out that my new friend was about to hitchhike across to my side of the island, and I willingly offered him a ride.

The day took on a surreal quality in which the long and usually tedious drive turned into a grand adventure. It started with Michael taking me for breakfast at his favourite roadside cafe, where the cook had me in fits of giggles. An ex-New Yorker with a filthy mouth, she slapped out cynical stand-up lines about her life as a sexually-bored housewife that had me crying with laughter.

When I confessed that I didn't enjoy driving on the windy, pot-holed roads, Michael immediately offered to drive, stopping to show me glorious views and special places that I would never have found on my own. To relieve the oppressive heat of the midday sun, he took me to a hidden swimming hole that was the epitome of a Hawaiian paradise. Diving off the rocks and swimming deep under the cobalt water, I experienced what I had come to the island for – a dropping away of the tension I had been carrying. By the time we reached Paia he had asked if he could take me out to dinner, and I registered that I enjoyed his company so much, I was starting to fancy him!

Michael was a real old-fashioned cowboy and a perfect gentleman. He opened my car door, put his jacket around my shoulders when it was chilly, and sang me love songs on his guitar. Because he was in his sixties I assumed that he would be sexually reserved – instead, we came together with a chemistry that blew all my fuses. After our first sexual encounter, I asked him incredulously: "*Where* did you learn to make love like that?" He laughed and, without missing a beat, answered in his American drawl, "Darlin', I've been a lover *all* my life."

We made love outside on warm star-lit nights and had picnics of fruit straight from the trees growing wild on the mountain sides. My house had an outdoor bathtub set in a tropical garden, where Michael tenderly washed my hair with a wild plant that actually lathered up when wet. It felt wonderful to be looked after; to be in the protective arms of a loving man again.

On Maui I attracted two of my soul family members to remind me that I was always supported. Michael was an old soul who had very obviously contracted to assist me in a time of need. And he introduced me to another elder of the community, a spunky woman in her seventies, Ruby, whom I loved instantly. She was like my mother in some ways, quite blunt, telling it like it is — admonishing me for wearing too much make-up or for over-analysing things. Like myself she had been inspired by *The Pleiadian Agenda* and the Marciniak books. It was a joy for her to meet a Pleiadian star sister in the little off-grid valley where she had chosen to spend her wisdom years.

One of the highlights of my time with Michael was a day spent in the crater of the majestic Haleakala volcano. Pele, the fire goddess of the island, called me to the fiery heart of her mountain, guiding our hike through the starkly beautiful landscape of orangey-red fire cinders and cones. Suspended above the clouds, rainbow bridges magically appeared before us and tiny fluorescent birds guided our way.

The temptation to prolong our affair after I left the island was undeniable, but we both knew that we were from different worlds, and that our time together was simply a precious gift. Michael was like the character Costas who seduces Shirley Valentine in the movie by the same name — a knight in shining armour whose mission on Earth was to love the women who were placed in his care. He reminded me how simple and easy it can be to share love.

Machu Picchu 2011   Mt Putucussi backdrop   The infamous rockslide

With the women of Cusco   In Bolivia: DebRa & Keenara to my right

Maui, Hawai: spot me in the banyan tree   With Ruby, my Pleiadian star-sister

CHAPTER 36

Mission Accomplished

My trip to Canada directly after Maui was very poignant. The groups of light tribe wherever I travelled were so grateful to meet each other, and to take part in the light work we were guided to accomplish. In the *Awakening your Light Body* course in White Rock, I channelled during the opening circle that each one present would receive healing in whatever form was appropriate to their process. What followed over the next three days was in fact a series of individual chakra activations, not at all like the other *Light Body* workshops I had led. My work had always been to empower others to become leaders where that was part of their chosen destiny, and this aspect was accelerating all the time. Students were stepping up to the mark as teachers in their own right – such a powerful thing to witness for both me and the other participants.*

Despite my restorative interlude in Hawaii and my successful workshops in Canada, I still felt like I was coming apart at the seams. The crying had not abated, my menopausal symptoms were off the scales, and I was unhappy in my temporary accommodation in London. To help me with an outside perspective, I decided to have a reading from Tatanka Nehweh, whose guidance I trusted implicitly.

Shortly into the session, her guides came right out with a shocker. They told me in no uncertain terms that my days as a Warrior of the Light were numbered, and that the 11.11.11 was in fact my final undertaking in this phase of my path. I was advised to stop travelling after the Sedona conference, to make home in London once more, and to look inwards in order to go through a vital period of personal healing.

---

* By 2011 I was teaching and healing extensively through the **12-13 chakra system** and the activation of our 'dormant' DNA. If this interests you, there are 3 free chakra webinars on my site, accompanied by a diagram illustrating this multi-dimensional model.

In many of my meditations you will hear reference to the **Cosmic Star Portal** at the top of your aura and the **Earth Star Portal** at the bottom of your aura – these are the first and last of the 12 energy centres. The **One-Heart** is the 13th chakra – superimposed upon the personal and higher hearts; our new 5th-dimensional heart centre.

This was a radical shift in thinking for me! I'd been propelled onto my mission as a Warrior of the Light in 2007, and believed that my commitment was until the December solstice of 2012. I wasn't expecting to be officially taken off duty thirteen months early! The shock was followed very shortly by a huge wave of relief. I craved some time and space to rethink my life. London certainly wasn't where I wanted to be in the long-term, but I needed to have a real home again, and to spend some quality time with my children. It all seemed to make sense.

My guides confirmed the validity of the advice, adding that it was time to gracefully let go of the warrior mind-set that had served me so well on my journey; time to surrender to my softer *yin*, receptive, goddess aspect. They explained that it was not a case of my spiritual quest being over; it was simply that I needed time-out to deal with my personal life and needs. I was at a transition point and could no longer continue with my mission and ignore my unhealed wounds. Embracing the change, I asked my webmaster to alter my website header from *Warrior of the Light* to *Goddess of the Light*.

I put one final mammoth effort into the manifestation of the 11.11.11 Sedona event that I had been guided to create: a free ceremony in which hundreds of people, including local indigenous leaders, were to converge around a medicine wheel formed in the wilderness of that powerful land. The ceremony would be followed by a two-day conference with several other speakers presenting alongside of me, including Aluna Joy Yaxk'in, Anrita Melchizedek and Gabrielle Young.*

This was to be a conference with a difference – consisting not only of talks or presentations, but also meditations and consciousness-raising techniques which required the participation of all 222 participants. The manifestation of the conference was the pinnacle of my mission – a super-human demonstration of what one person can accomplish when she gives herself in service to the human tribe. DebRa, KeenaRa, Ezeriel and other dear friends stepped forward to

---

* A beautiful meditation, in some ways an expanded version of the *Essential Daily Practices*, was given in the lead-up to the 11.11.11. It was called **Angelic Higher Self Activation**, and includes a visualisation of your own etheric angel wings unfurling from between your shoulder blades. It is a favourite with many of the light tribe – give it a try!

assist, and my own Gabriella Light Child was at my side throughout. No longer a child, she was given a new name on Cathedral Peak Vortex – *Zahara* – an identity that she is yet to fully embrace, as an activator of the tribe through the light transmissions of her beautiful voice. When I arrived back in London from Sedona, I had a massive sense of MISSION ACOMPLISHED! I was also on the verge of collapse.

The next chapter in my life was about to begin – the interval of personal enquiry and healing of which Tatanka's guides had spoken. In response to my reluctance to address the unhealed past, my Pleiadian friends reminded me as usual: *The Time Is Now.*

Activating a portal at Lake Louise: Light tribe at White Rock, Canada
singing *Om Neelama Shanti*

11.11.11 conference with DebRa & Gabby Zahara

Leading a dance

11.11.11 ceremony in Sedona: channelling and drumming in the medicine wheel

Our crystal and flower altar

CHAPTER 37

Healing the Past

To make my full-time return to London a more attractive proposition, I needed to come up with a plan that inspired me. Gabby and Max were by now in separate digs with friends, Jeremy was still in Portal Close, and I didn't want to live on my own. I decided to initiate a "conscious house-share," in order to attract a like-hearted community within the city.

I put the word out that I was looking for a large house with a garden to rent in the south-east, and that anyone drawn to living in a conscious community should step forward. Within a couple of months, I and three other women had joined forces to manifest a lovely home in Sydenham. I'd imagined that we would be a mixed group of five or six people, but the universe decided that we were to be four women, and so it was. I plunged into the project headlong, reclaiming some of the furniture from my old home and making the house beautiful. I started offering weekly meditation classes from the house in order to keep me connected with my old work, while not over-taxing me energetically.

When the dust had settled and the house was in order, I discovered exactly what my guides had meant about a period where I was forced to address my "unhealed wounds." I had a tendency to avoid *shadow work,* which involves uncovering and facing the pain that underlies dysfunctional behaviour patterns. For many years, I believed that all that was necessary to dissolve the dark, was to focus on the light. I now know that for most of us, this is unfortunately not so.

Some, like Eckart Tolle and the Buddha, are triggered spontaneously into a permanent Higher Self state of peace, where all past pain is instantly healed. But for the rest of us, when we hide from our pain, it will resurface in our lives one way or another in order to make us deal with it.

I was now living only a few miles away from Jeremy and his

new family, and the unresolved issues from our marriage suddenly slapped me right in the face. Six years after the end of my twenty-year relationship, I was faced with memories and feelings I had unconsciously suppressed – disappointments, frustrations, and the pain of being rejected by the man whom I had loved and supported unconditionally for so many years.

Jeremy had processed our break-up in the months and years immediately following our parting. I, on the other hand, had moved straight from the Higher Self "bubble" that propelled me painlessly through the separation, into the typical post-divorce boyfriends phase. Following swiftly on the heels of that exploration, my "Warrior of the Light" chapter was initiated, in which I surrendered unconditionally to my spiritual mission.

At the time of our separation, I was on a high where I saw only the positive side of everything. Looking back years later, I recognised that without the grace of the extraordinary Higher Self state I experienced during the transition, Jeremy and I would have struggled through years of arguments and pain. That outcome would undoubtedly have damaged the children psychologically, as well as causing a set-back in our own paths. I am eternally grateful for the assistance I received at that time, which resulted in a harmonious end to our marriage. Nevertheless, it came as a bit of a blow when I realised – six years down the line – that I still needed to go through a process of healing around the dissolution of our partnership!

When Jeremy and I split up, I trusted that my next partner was just around the corner – but the fact that he had not showed up as yet, forced me to look at my relationship history honestly. I already knew that my early relationships were based on the belief that this was the only avenue through which I could receive true love and support. At a very young age I had therefore started to confuse sex with love – in my experience they went hand-in-hand. And, as I experienced the potential to enter a state of bliss through sex from my very first encounters, it became a form of spiritual nourishment – although I wouldn't have voiced it that way at the time. For the beginning of this new healing journey – around sex and relationships – I was presented with a perfect series of synchronicities.

It began with a trip to Glastonbury one day, where I met an interesting man who happened to be a relationship counsellor. That same night, curious about him and his work, I googled his name. A video link popped on my screen with the title: "Do's and Don'ts in the Bedroom." As I watched it, my mouth literally dropped open – it was outrageously sexist and old fashioned! It was based on the concept of a man being "a real man" in the bedroom – in charge, confident, leading the way – while the woman was ideally feminine, more passive and receptive. Women were advised never to make the first move, to avoid being on top when making love, and not to be too athletic, noisy or directive in bed. I fell asleep completely nonplussed, wondering what century these people lived in.

The first thing that entered my head on waking was the video – and once again I rolled my eyes indignantly at how Stone Age it was. But the very next thought that popped into my mind was of a relationship I'd had at the age of nineteen, where I was almost exclusively on top when making love. I mulled it over for a while, concluding that it was the shyness and inexperience of the boyfriend in question that had led to my taking a dominant role. The minute I admitted to myself that the sexual dynamics in that relationship were dysfunctional, I thought of another boyfriend where the dynamic was very similar!

Oh yea, I thought, I was the one who initiated sex there as well; I was the one leading the way; in this second case, more or less teaching a socially inept man how to have a girlfriend. Why had I chosen that role – and how many times in my life had I done something similar? Suddenly the approach given in the video didn't seem so outrageous. It was old fashioned, sure, and there were elements with which I didn't agree – but I started to see how I had fallen into the trap of the "modern woman" who was often dominant, and who believed that being athletic and adventurous in bed was desirable.

I remembered Michael in Hawaii, and how much I had enjoyed being in the classical feminine role with him. He was the epitome of the old fashioned male protector and had made it easy for me to let him take the lead, especially as I had started our interaction allowing myself to be vulnerable and open. I questioned my heart about what I really wanted in my next relationship – about what my soul truly called for from a man – and it wasn't so far off from the concept outlined in the video. I wanted to be loved unconditionally and to feel protected in the arms of a strong man. I was ready to be softer and more receptive, letting go of the need to be in control.

Some of the concepts in the video were from the teachings of John Gray in *Men are from Mars, Women are from Venus,* a book I had never read. Naturally, as the universe was conspiring with me in this unfolding, my housemate happened to have a copy of this book on the shelf right outside my bedroom door. I started reading it immediately, and was transfixed by the advice given to women in the first chapter. The author asserts that men don't want to be changed or improved, even if you are doing it out of love – they just want to be accepted. Even offering a man help or advice can apparently make him feel weak or incompetent. I thought about the long list of "rescue operations" I'd embarked on in my partnerships, and cringed.

Now completely fascinated by what was unfolding, I sat at my desk and made a list of every single relationship in my life. I placed two columns besides the men's names with tick boxes for whether the relationship was functional (a) sexually and (b) in general. I wasn't judging the relationships as "good" or "bad" as such, because there were so many other factors to consider. My criterion in the exercise was simply to determine whether our roles had been as described in the video: the man in charge in a protective, dominant role, and myself in the receptive, feminine role. Very soon in the exercise I noted that the relationships where I was dominant or in rescue-mode, were nearly always relationships where I also led the way in bed.

All started well as I ticked both boxes in the affirmative through my early relationships, between the ages of fourteen and nineteen. My boyfriends over these years were strong, confident and charismatic, naturally leading the way. I responded by respecting them, allowing them autonomy and taking the receptive, feminine role; enjoying being protected by the man. Then there was an abrupt turn-around with hardly a single tick – from midway through my nineteenth year (my second year at university) – right through to the age of 53 in my brief relationship with Michael in Hawaii! I was completely dumfounded! Could this really be true, that I had reversed the natural polarity of the mating game for the overwhelming majority of my life? What had happened to change my behaviour so dramatically?

The answer was glaringly obvious. The pattern reversed after my heart was broken for the first time. Mark, the boyfriend in question, had been my whole life; my existence and happiness revolved solely around our union. I had not noticed any signs of his restlessness until the night he finished with me, and I had no resources upon which to call, because I had never been dumped before! I remember crying myself to sleep for months, utterly bereft of any desire to go on, sleep-walking my way through the final term of the university year.

The next man who attracted me was the first of many who were a safe bet – less confident and experienced than me – and, at the end of the day, not as likely to break my heart. Even at the point where I decided it was time to manifest a husband, I remember thinking that it wasn't crucial for me to be head-over-heels in love. My priority was that the man I married would love me and always be faithful; a good husband and a great father to our children – all of which Jeremy proved to be. I reflected on the first stage of our relationship where I had yet again shifted into rescue mode with a man who was younger than me and in need of some direction in life. It was obvious, in retrospect, that my subconscious belief was that if I were in charge, I would be less likely to be rejected.

At the completion of this mind-bending process, my affair in Hawaii assumed a new significance. As I knew from the inception that the relationship with Michael was temporary, and my hopes and dreams were therefore not invested, I allowed him to take charge from the very beginning. In fact, I allowed him to take the lead both on an everyday level, *and* in bed. It had been a huge relief, in fact, to let go of the need to be in control – and it had led to this moment in my life where I could call on my experience with him as an example that it was possible. I had shed light on the pain that had been the root cause of my tendency to compromise in relationships, and was therefore able to re-set my paradigm for my future. Shadow work wasn't so bad after all.

There was another step that was necessary to heal my past with Jeremy. It came about when, on my return to London after a holiday, my body suffered an acute crisis the minute the plane set wheels on English soil. I developed an excruciating toothache, and to make matters even worse, my lower back gave way so severely that I was practically immobilised. Although the dentist surgery was within a fifteen-minute walk of my home, I travelled there by taxi because my lower back was in such agony. After the offending tooth with a long-term infection had been extracted, I hobbled to a nearby coffee shop to recover from the anaesthetic. Hardly able to sit because of the pain in my sacrum, I closed my eyes and connected in with my guides, asking what was necessary to heal the pain. The answer came thus:

> We are with you, dear one. This is part of your process of healing the past. We ask you to sit now and remember the life you have lived in this city – to remember the joy, the sense of achievement, the laughter and fun that was there as you proceeded through the years of your marriage and child-bearing. Treasure each memory as it arises; send love and gratitude to all those who surface in your memories, and it will be done.

I was puzzled about how this might help my back, but what the Star Councils were suggesting sounded simple enough. Sitting in the coffee shop, I closed my eyes and directed my thoughts back to my early years in London, which I usually remembered as difficult, and found vignettes in picture form of memories that I could appreciate. I remembered new friends that had been kind; the joy of getting my first massage job; the laughter I shared with the eight-year-olds when I teaching. A memory surfaced of a schoolgirl who had told me on the day I left, with tears in her eyes, "I will never forget you Miss, I've never met anyone like you." I thought back on the parties we hosted in our first, humble flat; the fun I had making feasts out of scraps; the barge holiday we had shared with friends on a canal; watching rugby in the pub with the locals.

Similar to one of my ayahuasca journeys, my mind was transformed into a cinema, memories playing out in chronological order, affording me the opportunity to forgive and let go of pain, through the magical formula of undiluted gratitude. With my focus on treasuring each memory, I realised how distorted our memory of the past becomes when we are disillusioned by the outcome. I re-lived the wonder of childbirth and not the difficulty; the joys of motherhood rather than the frustrations; the love and support I received for so many years from Jeremy, rather than the pain of being rejected.

I became utterly transported through this process, unaware of where I was or how much time had gone by. When I snapped back into the present and opened my eyes, I was stunned to find that over an hour had passed. My Earl Grey tea and carrot cake sat untouched on the café table before me. Disorientated, I jumped up to go to the bathroom, discovering in the mirror that the top of my t-shirt was sopping wet and covered with mascara stains. I had evidently been crying profusely – which explained why all the other customers had moved so far away from me!

On my way home I suddenly remembered that I'd caught a taxi to the dentist. Why had I done that when it was only a fifteen-minute walk from home? And then it hit me – I had not been able to walk! My back pain had one hundred percent disappeared. The exercise of gratitude that I had just completed, reliving my twenty-five or so years in London through a new filter of appreciation, had totally healed my back pain! Fresh tears of joy spurted from my eyes at the realisation of the deep healing that had just taken place.

When we choose gratitude over dissatisfaction, compassion over resentment, the result will always be healing. When we find a way to truly accept, honour and forgive ourselves and all others involved, the past is integrated peacefully into our psyche and stops causing discomfort. Love is the always the way.

CHAPTER 38

Completions

Back in the garden of England in 2012, after a period of rest and recuperation, I once again heard the call of the Avebury-Stonehenge-Glastonbury portal that had been so pivotal in my awakening. I was bored and restless in London, and decided to offer a couple of workshops out on the land to introduce more of the tribe to the beauty of these power portals.

At that juncture, I believed that when I had been taken "off-duty" as a Warrior of the Light, my obligations after the 11.11.11 had been nullified. In the process of my first 2012 workshop in Avebury, however, I was snapped back into an acute awareness of my original commitment to the Winter Solstice 2012 – and of the whole purpose of the preceding five years of Gaia-and-Tribe Reconnection projects. The crystals we had buried in the stone circle, the intense activations of portals and light grids, were all part of a larger mission that was yet to be completed!

The directions I had earlier received when my guides first introduced the Avebury Healing Project in 2007, was that on the day of the 2012 solstice, I should gather a huge crowd of our light tribe to surround the embankment of the Avebury Stone Circle. We were to tone into the centre, accompanied by gongs, didgeridoos and other frequency shifters, in order to reconnect the light grid which was above the circle. Our work was to be assisted by the energy coming in from Stonehenge – where Armukara was committed to continue working, and Glastonbury – where Urtema was stationed to open a portal on the day. Finally, we were instructed to place a huge Lemurian "record-keeper" crystal in the centre of the circle, which would subsequently be buried, forever holding the new energies in coherence.

When I arrived home after the Avebury tour, I located and re-read the original transmission I had received. The conclusion read:

There is a Star of David to be activated in the British landscape – which aligns with Egypt; with South Africa and Table Mountain; with Peru and Machu Picchu; and with Palenque in Mexico. These places are to be activated and healed by you and all who are called to the mission. The purpose in Avebury is not only the healing of the stone circle, but it is to unite a band of light workers through love. Solara, you are called to unite bands of light workers through love and united purpose and intention.

Amazed, it dawned on me that I had actually been preparing for this event through *all* of the work I had done over the five intervening years. I had been to *all* of the power places listed in this message and had undeniably been continuously *uniting bands of Light Workers through love and united purpose and intention*. I really had no choice but to honour my initial pledge to lead the 2012 Avebury ceremony.

In 2011 my guides had told me that my work was not over, but that I was simply relinquishing the warrior role in order to recover my physical and emotional balance. It had been necessary for me to *believe* that I was letting go of all responsibilities, simply to get me to focus on my personal healing. When my reconnection with the 2012 project occurred spontaneously, I was able to handle it in a different way – by being softer, more receptive to being assisted, and more in the flow.

In the lead-up to the solstice, I was inspired to hold an all-day event for the 12.12.12 in Glastonbury Town Hall. Part workshop, part celebration, it was undisputedly my favourite gathering in that momentous year. There was such an atmosphere of celebration and excited anticipation in the air. For many people, the years preceding 2012 had been underlain with a tension around what would actually happen on the "end-date" of the Mayan Calendar: the 21st of December 2012. But the large group attracted into our circle that day were one hundred percent *with the program* of faith and not doubt; love and not fear. My beautiful soul sister Urtema guided the group alongside me as I celebrated with my soul family, drumming and dancing into the night.

In the days leading up to the solstice in Avebury, a freezing wind and sleety rain made it all but impossible to prepare the gathering crowds for the event. When we ventured out of the shelter of our meeting room, the rain slashed mercilessly into our faces, and we were forced to withdraw to the shelter of the Red Lion pub. For three days leading up to the ceremony, we affirmed: "We will be graced by Father Sun at the solstice!"

When the big day finally dawned, we were greeted by the glorious site of bright blue skies and streaming sunshine. Within a few hours the mid-winter sun had dried the puddles and muddy fields, and we gathered jubilantly in the south east quadrant to begin our work. Before we spread out to surround all four quadrants of the great circle, the Councils of Light gave us their blessing and encouraged us to act as one unit; to stay coherent as a group throughout the day. We took our places on the embankments, ready to sing and tone our hearts out, visualising the portal opening above the circle. Didgeridoo and gong players accompanied us, the deep vibrations of their sound merging with our voices, flowing through the ancient stones and into the point above us, where our concentration was focussed. This day will forever be etched into the hearts of those who joined together in ceremonies across the globe, to co-create our new future and re-set the destiny of Earth.

Much to my joy, both Max and Gabby were by my side, in the very place where we had planted the 44 crystals in the original Gaia-and-Tribe Reconnection. It was so healing to bring the project to completion with this ceremony. I felt an overwhelming relief at having seen the whole mission through, from its inception at the Stone of Initiation in 2007, to the manifestation of this glorious day.

I was passing the baton onto a new band of Light Warriors – amongst others to Katy Tucker, a faithful student for many years who had committed to overseeing the burial of the central connector crystal in the circle after the initial event. I had read in one of the other Solara's books about "first wavers and second wavers." The first wave of light workers had stepped up to lead the way in Earth's reawakening in the sixties, seventies and eighties, and – after many years of dedication – had come to a place where they handed the baton on to a new wave of enthusiastic leaders. At the time that I read this, I knew that I was second waver – but I now felt myself passing the leadership staff onto a whole new generation of warriors, and Katy was one of these – perhaps part of a third wave which had been initiated in the lead-up to 2012. I had witnessed many other students over the years stepping into their power through the teachings of the Councils of Light.

There was another completion that was necessary in the months that followed, which was to visit my homeland once more. I had not been to South Africa since my Pleiadian-Sirian activations of 2007, and I heard the familiar call: *The Time Is Now!*

Nearly every major event in my spiritual path has been on or around the March equinox. When my journey with the Pleiadian and Sirian Star Councils was initiated in March 2007, my life had accelerated so radically, it was like being sucked into a tornado. As the Spring Equinox of 2013 dawned exactly six years later, I felt the need to gain a new perspective on what had happened on my path, and why. I set two important intentions for the trip – first, to reconnect with my family and roots, and second, to revisit the power places that had triggered a new beginning for me in 2007.

I spent my first week in Johannesburg with my eldest sister Gail who, although she loved me dearly, had never come even close to understanding my spiritual work. Her feelings about my life and work she summed up in one word: *weird.* This trip was very different from previous stays with her as she was between jobs, and therefore had more time to spend with me. I had several requests for one-on-one sessions while I was in Johannesburg, and Gail readily agreed to let me see clients at her house.

Meeting the people who came for sessions triggered her curiosity about exactly what I was doing. She could see the difference in my clients before and after, and questioned me in detail about what had happened. For the first time ever, Gail could relate to the purpose of making a connection with the invisible worlds. When I channelled for her, at her request, the encouragement and greater perspective she received from my guides touched her deeply. It was so joyful for me to have my spiritual path accepted by one of my family.

When I moved onto Knysna to join my other sister, Darrell, Gail's son surprised us all by paying for his mum to fly there as well, so that we three sisters could spend a few days together. It was fifteen years since we had been reunited, and there was a certain amount of apprehension in all of us about how we would get on. Our worries were groundless, and the time we spent together was incredibly therapeutic. We visited places on the magnificent salt water lagoon where we had holidayed as children, and all three of us could feel the presence of our mom and dad, smiling at our reunion. We recognised this opportunity for family healing, having fun with each other as adults, without the tension that had so often been present with our parents.

The day finally arrived on which I was to revisit the Knysna forests where I had received my first Pleiadian and Sirian activations. My guides told me that on this second visit to Spitzkop and the Big Tree, I would be able to integrate what had taken place since then and would simultaneously be coded for my future purpose – to "remember my Star Nation's lore" – a reference, I believe, to the channelled book that follows the one that you are now reading.

I opened my eyes on the day of the expedition with a strange uneasiness beating in my heart. This increased in the car after I took the Uniondale turnoff that led through an African township. A group of teenagers appeared out of nowhere, running and shouting beside my car in a threatening manner. Startled, I pushed my foot down and left them behind in the dust, bumping along the rough dirt road, bordered by thick pine forests on either side. My memory of the previous drive was of pretty, dappled sunlight filtering through the trees – but this time the sun was hidden behind a solid bank of black clouds stretched across the horizon. The rain commenced very suddenly in typical African style, pelting down through claps of lightning and roaring thunder.

I stopped on the side of the road for a time and considered turning back, filled with trepidation. I needed to pull myself together! Closing my eyes, I centred myself, tuned in, and was told that I was simply manifesting outward signs of my anxiety concerning what I might be told about my future. I was firmly instructed to remove the fear from my energy body, and move into trust. As I had done so many times before, I went through the steps of the *Essential Daily Practices* meditation, which includes the command, "Let all energy I have given away or left behind, return to me NOW!" Calmer, and fully grounded, I continued on my way, finally pulling into the layby for the King Edward VII Big Tree just as the downpour abated.

At the Big Tree, sitting in the exact location where I had received the Pleiadian activation, tears rolled down my cheeks as I channelled this message from my beloved star friends:

> Your mission over these preceding years has been to assist in the awakening of humanity – and in this you have succeeded. You have accomplished a unique service to your tribe, through demonstrating fearlessness and through bringing forth our guidance and assistance. Now, as you stand in your original place of ignition, you receive – rather than activation – the *healing of Great Mother*. Allow yourself to receive the healing energy of the Mother and of the tree beings that surround you. Gaia is grateful for your work – She assists in your healing now. All that is necessary for you to come to a place of vitality, strength, health and joy is in perfect timing. Be at peace now, dear one, with this completion. Be at peace and rest, assured that your work has been well done. Waves of love we send to you now, and to all those on Earth who transition.

Tears flowed as I felt the healing energy of completion flood
my being. It was time to move onto my final destination of Spitzkop.
As I climbed the hill, a blanket of mist swirled around me, covering
me with goose bumps. I huddled under the bushes at the heart of the
hill and was joined once again by the Sirians:

> The Sirian Brotherhood of the Light speaks through
> you once more. You have been joined by many
> groups of star nations and ancient entities on your
> journey, and have accomplished your assignments
> as given. Once on your mission to assist with the
> en-lightenment of the people, the joy from your
> successes, and the love you received from those you
> helped, over-shadowed all else. As a result of this,
> your strong will and determined nature led you to
> take on more than we, your guides, asked of you.
>
> Your choice, to be of service at the expense
> of all else personal, was a result of your pain
> and isolation on the earth planet. Like so many
> others who choose to be Emissaries of Light,
> your experience of harmony and unity in the
> other dimensions contrasted so harshly with the
> separation and despair prevalent on Earth, that
> any sacrifice was considered worthwhile in order to
> lessen that gap.
>
> Thus have you come to a place where peace
> and quiet are essential for the recovery of your
> health and happiness. You have no choice but to be
> *in the now* – your future is recalibrating itself as we
> speak. Each decision made in each now-moment
> affects where your soul leads you. Over and over
> will you re-focus on your heart's true desires, so
> that the universe can work with you, supporting
> you in the new life that comes.

This information was crucial in helping me to understand where I had stepped out of alignment on my path. Ever since my uncontrollable crying had kicked in during my second Peru trip, I had harboured a nagging and uncomfortable suspicion that following the the Star Councils' guidance during those several years had contributed to the melt-down I had endured. I somehow blamed them for putting me on path that was too accelerated for me to cope with.

As I reflected on the message, I realised that in the years immediately following my 2007 activations, I had always planned my workshops in accordance with the guidance I received. In later years, however, I had sometimes been responding to what the *public* was asking of me, and *not* what my guides were advising. At various junctures I had been persuaded to offer, for instance: another sacred trip to Peru; an extra *Opening to Channel* workshop; a further visit to the US. In my efforts to please everyone, I had indeed "taken on more than my guides had asked of me."

My natural talent for manifesting, combined with my desire to be of service, had taken over. I had also subconsciously been dissolving my loneliness in the vessel of love that was always present when I worked with a group. These recognitions were vital for me to finally make peace with the conclusion of my *Warrior* path.

Back in the shelter of my London home, I looked at my website and realised that not only was the *Warrior of the Light* title no longer relevant, I didn't feel comfortable with any label. I didn't want or need the title of *Goddess of the Light* – I was simply Solara An-Ra, one of the light tribe. My confused webmaster, no doubt thinking that this chick was suffering from a severe identity crisis, agreed to yet another header change on my website: *Light Tribe of Gaia*. I re-set my intentions in alignment with my new understanding of what I needed, to continue to create the space necessary for my rebalancing, so that the universe and I could co-create a delightful new chapter in the ongoing book of my life.

12.12.12 in Glastonbury   Winter Solstice 2012 in Avebury

Channelling in the centre of the circle before moving to the embankments

CHAPTER 39

The Call of the White Isle

M y shared home in London, much like any new relationship, went
through a honeymoon phase, followed shortly by a more gritty,
reality-bites period. Within a few short months we discovered that our
individual motivations for living together were worlds apart. We hadn't
drawn up many guidelines for our house-share, other than agreeing
not to have a TV, to be vegetarian and to share regular meditations
and talking-stick circles. Within a few months, I found myself in what
felt like a regular city house-share, where the occupants went off to
work every day, spending most of their free time closeted in their own
rooms. It wasn't the nurturing environment of which I had dreamed.

During my first year of living full-time in London again, I felt
the purpose of being there. I rested, spent time with my children,
healed my past with Jeremy, and completed my contract with the
2012 portal. I was still, however, intermittently experiencing deep
isolation and loneliness. I tried to rebuild my social life through the
participants of my meditation circles and the One-Spirit gatherings
where I offered channelled guidance to the tribe, but I never managed
to replace the social circle that had dissolved along with my marriage.

London people are always busy, wrapped up in their own
lives. I saw loneliness all around me – hundreds of thousands of
people going about their daily tasks like zombies. In the tea shops or
internet cafes, on the bus or tube, very few people smiled or started
conversations with each other. A culture of separation stared me in
the face every day.

One night in early 2013, abruptly wide awake at 3 a.m., I felt
myself descending down the dreaded tunnel into depression. I was
lost; everything felt pointless; and I had no idea what to do to change
up a gear. I had been on strike from channelling for a while – I was
tired and I didn't want any new missions – I just wanted to lead a
normal life. But needs must. I did the *Daily Practises* and connected

with my guides, simply shouting "Help!" I knew that they were always standing by, aware of my predicament, so there seemed no point in elaborating.

I felt their amusement as they instructed me to pretend that I was a client who had come to see me for therapy. I was apparently able to "therapize" myself out of the hole. "Thanks a lot!" I responded sarcastically – but I could see the humour in the situation. Because I was on strike with my guides and didn't want to be told what to do, I was being given the option to receive help simply through channelling my therapist self.

I picked up my notebook, putting myself in the role of the therapist, tuned in and wrote, "Solara, I understand that you are unhappy about several different things in your life right now. Tune into your heart and tell me, what is the one thing that needs to change first, in this moment?" The answer came out instantaneously, with no hesitation: *London.* I was amazed at how easy this was! It was evident to me that I was in fact channelling my Higher Self in two different aspects: Solara the therapist and Solara the client. The questions came so spontaneously, and the answers so definitively, that there was no room to doubt the process.

I looked at the answer: *London.* So I needed to leave London – it was suddenly as obvious and as clear as day. Could I really leave, I asked myself, having made the commitment to live closer to my children? *Yes, I could.* I had spent the last year and a half in the city and was no longer anxious about them needing my support on an everyday level. I also *knew* that they would prioritise my happiness over my presence in London. It was time for the next question.

"What are your priorities, Solara, in choosing your new home?" Once again, the answer came out lightning fast, this time with three phrases:

1. Somewhere more sunny, at the ocean

2. Somewhere more hippy; more friendly

3. Somewhere not too far from the children

Analysing these priorities, I knew immediately that my new

home would be in Europe. This is how my children would be able to visit me easily. I had never even considered moving to anywhere on the coast in Europe, especially not to a non-English speaking country. But my heart opened effortlessly in this process, a knowing of the validity of this guidance running through every atom of my being. It felt like the therapy process was at an end and I had been given the clues I needed.

I came up with three possibilities and wrote them down in my book – *France, Portugal* and *Spain*. When I considered France in more depth, a distasteful shiver ran down my spine. No way was anywhere in France "hippy and friendly" – I crossed it out firmly. I mulled over the second option, Portugal. This felt more promising. I knew that that you could buy a farm quite cheaply in Portugal and I was soon to receive a bit of money from the sale of our house. With this thought, Gabby Zahara came to mind. She was passionate about improving her Spanish and had spoken for some years about living in a Spanish speaking country. I instinctively knew she would hate it if I moved to Portugal. "Oh well," I thought "I guess it must be Spain!" I circled *Spain* and promptly fell into a deep and peaceful sleep, my pen still in my hand.

I was awoken the next morning unreasonably early by a phone call from my gorgeous yoga teacher and friend Carole, who I hadn't seen for several years. "Hey Ca, I think I'm moving to Spain!" I declared as soon as my sleepy brain came into focus. "To Ibiza?" she asked excitedly. I told her that I hadn't considered Ibiza because it was notorious for alcohol, drugs and clubbing. She informed me that there was another side to the island entirely – a spiritual side that attracted many outsiders to live in the tranquil countryside of the north. She added that she'd always wanted to retire there and develop a retreat centre.

As I made my way downstairs for a cup of tea a few minutes later, I registered the words *Ibiza* and *retreat* from our conversation. For some years I had harboured a dream of living in a home big enough to house students who came for workshops or on retreat.

Simultaneously, I remembered a future vision my ex-boyfriend Brendan had received in 2007, in which I was running an establishment he jokingly nick-named "Solara's Psychic B&B." He said that some guests would stay a couple of days in order to have a session with me, while others would come to formally take part in a workshop or retreat. According to him, this place would become very well-known. Goosebumps covered my arms as I thought about this prediction.

Now in the kitchen, I greeted one of my housemates with the statement: "Hey, guess what? I think I'm moving to Ibiza!" "Aaaah, I'll be so jealous," she replied. "I've always dreamed of setting up a retreat centre in Ibiza." The penny was starting to drop that something significant was in process. I became suspended in the now moment where every detail was accentuated. Within an hour, a third person had said the words *Ibiza* and *retreat* in the same sentence.

I was totally ignorant about the island, didn't know a soul who lived there and had zero Spanish skills. But I *always* trust signs that come in threes, and I am notoriously impetuous. I phoned my family and friends that same afternoon and announced that I was moving to Ibiza. My children reacted with delighted surprise and approval – what young adults wouldn't want a mum who lived in Ibiza, one of the coolest holiday destinations in Europe? My friends and clients, used to my sudden changes of lifestyle by this time, rolled their eyes and muttered about why *I* got to live on a Mediterranean island. No one tried to talk me out of it, as it had become increasingly obvious that I was never going to settle happily in the city again.

From that day until the day I set foot on the island, the spirit of Ibiza floated in my consciousness – in my dreams and in my waking hours. Her ruling goddess, Tannit, called to me; her oceans sang to me; her pine-clad hills and cliff paths called to my walking boots. As soon as I had tied up the loose ends of my life, I packed my car with as much stuff as I could fit in, and began the mammoth journey to the White Isle.

CHAPTER 40

Magic Weaver

During my first summer on Ibiza, I soaked up the sun, lay for hours immersed in the ocean, joined an ecstatic dance group, and made friends from all corners of the globe. I felt my heart's desires manifested almost overnight. I was living at the ocean on a beautiful island that was indeed "more sunny, more hippy and friendly," and so easily accessible from London that my children could visit me at any time.

When I first arrived on the island, I was uncertain as to whether I wanted to do my old work or be known as a channel – it seemed like a perfect opportunity to reinvent myself and my life. But as 2014 dawned, it was made crystal clear that my time of teaching was not yet over. Only when I connected in with my guides again and began to share my gifts with the Ibiza light tribe, did my life flow with ease and grace. The Star Councils, overjoyed that I was ready to use my gifts once more, said:

> Within your third eye you hold, dear one, codes that are awakened and will assist others, seen and unseen. Just as Babaji transmits vibration through the Himalayan light grid, so will you transmit vibration through the grid that connects the Balearic Islands into the fields of Earth. Some of this will be private work and some will be witnessed by those who join you on the island. You will follow our guidance here as you have done before, and we will assist in aligning your frequencies with those of Gaia in this place. You will find a new way of being, and those who visit you on the island will be deeply affected.

I was also advised by my guides that I was now in the more mellow *Magic Weaver* phase of my life, where I could manifest results just as powerful without trying so hard – merely by being playful, creative and spontaneous.*

I soon discovered that when I tried to force things, *Warrior*-style, the island spat my attempts back in my face in a rather unpleasant way. Conversely, when I surrendered and went with the flow, everything fell into place effortlessly. It was, in fact, only after I had suffered several setbacks and totally given up on the idea of creating a retreat centre, that the right house literally fell into my lap. Against all odds, I manifested a perfect six-bedroomed villa, with a living room large enough to use as a workshop space, at an affordable rent. The location was ideal – only six minutes' drive from a town with all conveniences, while still immersed in the tranquillity which the north of the island still exudes. All-importantly, the Ibizenco owner was happy to draw up a long-term contract, and was totally open to my plans to develop the property.

The house was set in an ancient agricultural valley where the farmers still knocked the olives off the trees with wooden poles, collecting them in a blanket to take home and press themselves. The property included a grove of orange trees backed by a wild field, which was a perfect site for a yoga platform. I added solar panels on the roof, a yurt for extra accommodation, outdoor showers and a compost toilet. My friend Ernesto stepped in to establish an organic vegetable garden and to help me develop the neglected land surrounding the house into a magical garden.

The fact that the house was unfurnished in no way intimidated me. It gave me free reign to infuse the blank white canvass of a modern Spanish villa with the character and beauty of a sacred space. The store-room and extra kitchen at the back of the house provided the perfect space to make my own self-enclosed studio and garden – a sanctuary to which I could retreat when I needed time-out.

---

* Listen to the channelled message: **'The 3 Paths of Humans'** on my YouTube channel. Most of us move between 'Warrior of the Light,' 'Magic Weaver' & 'Frequency Keeper' roles.

The money from the sale of Portal Close came through in perfect timing for me to make these crucial investments in the centre. Miraculously, only a few months after signing the contract, *Casa Solara* was up and running as a retreat and community centre in the Summer of 2014. Ernesto, sent by the angels to support the project, moved into the yurt and began cooking for group retreats; teaching through example how to practise karma yoga or selfless service.

Shortly after setting up the centre I was guided to open an inter-dimensional portal in the meditation room – and from that moment on, emails poured in from teachers who wanted to hold retreats, and guests who want to spend time in the healing frequencies of the casa. The house attracts the perfect people at the perfect time for their awakening and life's unfolding. It is a magnet for soul star family groups, who attract each other in order to activate, support and learn from each other.

Thus began a new phase of my life, which is undeniably a version of the *psychic B&B* prophesied by Brendan. To my delight, I have discovered that it is possible to live in a community without living in a commune! I am in service in a new and soul-nourishing way, offering meditation classes, community potluck lunches, mantra singing circles and ashram-experience days to serve the Ibiza light tribe. I also lead workshops and Samadhi-Bliss Retreats with the assistance of my beloved Babaji. But I am aware that I am in a completion phase and that there is a change on the horizon.

I desire a quieter life in the future, when I am no longer running the centre and am serving through writing and transmissions to the greater tribe more than through teaching in person. My heart's desire is that Casa Solara will be sponsored, so that it may endure as a hub of light for the community long after I have let go of my many responsibilities here.

"And what of a beloved?" you ask. What is the conclusion of all the sexual and relationship healing I have shared with you? If I had known when I let go of Jeremy that I would be without a partner for so many years, I would probably have stepped off the planet – so strong was my pattern of feeling incomplete without a soulmate. Now that I have been single for what feels like an eternity, I believe that I have finally healed my past, and am free to embark on a new journey of relationship. I asked my guides recently if I would definitely have another partner in this lifetime, and they said:

> You are *in* the flow of this manifestation, and the *time is now* in which we celebrate with you the union with a beloved, who has waited for as long as you to fulfil this contract. Your union is destined in the stars; it is not – like others you have experienced – contracted within this 3-D existence. Rather, it is decreed from the dimensions of light and sound, where souls recognise each other through vibration and soul purpose.

I am aware that my "story" is only a *leela* – a play or dream that I am co-creating. This leela has no conclusion, and can change channels at any time, when it is decided for my highest good that my path lies elsewhere. What can we each do but serve life, and watch as the universe returns our generosity with a voluptuous serving of the same. What can we do but live each moment to its fullest capacity, striving to heal our lives through appreciation of each gift life brings.

As this book comes to completion I experience a realignment within my soul. The contract I made with my Pleiadian friends is fulfilled. It is not that I will desist from transmitting their loving messages to Earth's people – but my inner knowing is that *phase one* is complete.

When one makes a sacred contract it *must* play out one way or another. If we place obstacles in the way of its fulfilment through fear or laziness – or resistance in any of its expressions – we experience pain. If we drive through our resistance, opening into the flow of the divine will, we experience grace. Like naughty children, defiantly pushing against boundaries, challenging the laws that govern life, we test the waters in both directions. But finally, we must choose peace. We pay attention to what behaviours, what beliefs, result in pain – and we choose the other path.

Brothers and sisters of the light, search your hearts now for where you are not in alignment with the contract that you made – for each and every one of you *made an agreement to come to Earth at this time in order to serve in the transition.* You are presented with an opportunity, right here, right now, to re-member this sacred agreement – to re-seed Unity Consciousness on Gaia.

There is only one way to manifest unity on this planet – to *feel it from your own centre* – and to see, through the eyes of love, the love and light within each other. You can no longer divide yourselves into separate tribes – through your ideologies, your religions, or your cultures – YOU ARE ONE TRIBE!

Feel this truth within your heart. Separate yourself not from any other. The pain that comes from separation is deep and wounding – a wound in all parts of your psyche. There is only one path to happiness, and on that path, you forgive all others any perceived wrongs. You allow yourself to *feel what is real.* The time is now TO BE REAL, to acknowledge the beauty of your true self, to heal, to truly *live* and to open your heart fully.

From my One-Heart to yours – until we meet again –

I bid you farewell, with so much love.

Solara An-Ra, Magic Weaver for Gaia

Leading a ceremony at the power spot of Es Vedra

With my precious friends Pete & Kinan, initiators of Ibiza Planetary Meditations

Casa Solara

Ibiza tight tribe after a *Chamber of Light* activation

Marco & Beatrice leading kirtan

Ernesto (right) in the kirtan

Early morning yoga

Community potluck lunch

Meditation circle in the portal meditation room

The Councils of Light Speak

In this cosmic moment of time, remember what life is all about, dear ones. It is about a much grander scheme of things, in which all beings are united in a cosmic play that is unfolding. You are not pawns in this play; you are chosen ones. You have skills and knowledge beyond your present imaginings. Begin to see light as it is manifest in all things. See joy as it is manifest in all things. Learn to focus your minds and receptive senses so that what you input into them is carefully chosen, with discernment. When this skill is honed, you will be able to distance yourself from the things that are unimportant – and therefore have more energy to input that which is uplifting, and which keeps you to your purpose.

The Soul Star Portal within your chakric system radiates out infinitely when you are connected, attracting your soul star family into your reality. Waves of higher frequency stimulate it further when the prana tube is activated. The focus on prana tube activation cannot be underestimated at this time – it is your energetic pathway to union with the Cosmic Bliss through the Cosmic Star Portal, and true oneness with your planet through the Earth Star Portal. It is the means of interface with all dimensions within your galaxy.

Many have astral travelled out of their physical bodies into the other spheres. But the opportunity is presented to you now to access these spheres through your consciousness, while staying fully grounded into your bodies. With the reconnection of the 12 chakra system, humans experience the other worlds simply by looking within. In this context, meditation takes on a new meaning. No longer is the aim of going inwards simply to still the monkey-mind and reach a place of stillness. Now is the time to gaze inwards in order to connect with the universe, the galaxy, the stars, the sun, the earth and the core crystal. We take you into this experience with the Cosmic Connection Meditation now.

Cosmic Connection Meditation*

lose your eyes, and sit with a relaxed but aligned spine, in a chair or
on the floor. *Smile* as you sit there, your hands relaxed and open,
shifting into the crystalline frequency of gratitude. Start to perceive
the unconditional love of the Creator all around you, entering into
your energy field, and now into your physical body. Accept this love
now. It is a soft but bright pink light, entering your field now, and you
accept it joy-fully, grace-fully, unconditionally. Say out loud:

I am loved; I am be-loved; I am worthy.

Feel yourself opening to receive; opening to accept the love
of Source; knowing that you are a blessed child of the universe. And
the love of the Creator is your fundamental point of reference, your
reason for existence. Your crown chakra opens now, in unison with
the Cosmic Star Portal chakra at the top of your aura, as you receive
the loving, activating, enlightening power of Source into your being.

Now, bring your awareness to our beautiful planet, below your
body. You are sitting on her body, and also IN her energy field. Feel
overwhelming love and gratitude for your true mother opening within
you and pouring through a grounding cord that starts in your belly
and connects down, into the central heart of the Great Mother. Say
out loud:

I am one with Gaia. I am a part of her; she is a part of me.

You re-member your connection with your planet now, in your
every cell; in every atom of your be-ing. Your blood is singing the song
of Earth; your cells are vibrating with her frequency; remembering
their home. As you pour your love into her body, she pours her love
into you, and you light up with the radiance of her loving, healing,
creative power. Your prana tube is now active, a crystalline energy
tube running through all 12 chakras, plugged into the Great Central

---

* The recording of this meditation is available on Solara's website & YouTube channel.

Sun at the heart of your Milkyway galaxy; plugged into the core crystal of Gaia. You have opened this energy channel through your love for the Creator and your love for planet Terra. You have opened this all-important channel through your acceptance of love from Source and Mother Earth. When your hearts are open in love and gratitude – and you allow the love of the Creator and of Gaia to be received into your bodies – you activate your energetic pathway of union with them, and thereby, your multi-dimensionality.

This is easy, is it not? We are gifting you with a method to maintain your connection, your power, and the flow of abundance and grace in your life – simply by opening to receive love; and by opening to give love and honour to the two-way source of your existence with every breath.

Watch your breath now – the key way into your consciousness, and feel how you are able to draw light and sustenance from above and below – from the Cosmic Star Portal at the top of your aura, the energy streams through into your heart. From the Earth Star Portal at the bottom of your aura, the energy of the Core Crystal streams up into your heart. And you are the centre of the universe, floating in a sea of energy that unites all things. You are able to connect with all-that-is through your heart-felt desire to experience unity consciousness.

Love opens codes within your greater light body now, as your 12 chakras spin simultaneously to the right; 12 vortices spinning in unison, igniting the One-Heart now – your fifth-dimensional heart chakra. When you open yourself in love and gratitude for all-that-is, you take your rightful place as co-creators in the *Divine Plan for Gaia,* acting as channels for the energies of both Source and Gaia. Your prana tube spontaneously activates, and you gradually become aware of your true nature, remembering your true purpose. Say out loud:

I let go of all resistance to change. I am a co-creator in the Divine Plan for Ascension of Gaia. I am a channel for the energies of Heaven onto Earth

And so it is, dear ones; and so it is.

From our One-Heart to yours, Namaste.

Made in the USA
San Bernardino, CA
13 February 2018